To Van & Fawonda
Green

Don Humphus
6-30-92
at RR
Philemon 6

Hearts .On Fire

Hearts On Fire

A Strategy for Dynamic Evangelism

"I pray that you may be active in sharing your faith."
Philemon 6

Don Humphrey

Gospel Advocate Co.
P. O. Box 150
Nashville, TN 37202

Hearts On Fire

Copyrighted © 1990 by Don Humphrey

ISBN 0-89225-409-2

Acknowledgements

Not all of the ideas in this book are original with me. Many of the thoughts and ideas on this subject have been collected over a lifetime. I can't footnote many of the ideas that I know aren't mine, because I don't have any way of remembering where I got them, but I am indebted to all of these speakers and authors through the years who have contributed to my learning.

I am also indebted to Nelson Eddy, Ancil Jenkins, Richard Jones, Mary Hollingsworth, Clayton Pepper, Jay Reynolds, Bob Rielly, Randy Simmons, Don Umphrey and Flavil Yeakley, Jr., who have read the manuscript and contributed valuable suggestions. Edwin White and Paul Methvin have given me a lot of encouragement to develop the material and provided opportunities for me to present it.

I am most indebted to Bob Stewart, who has edited the material for me so that I appear to be a much better author than I really am.

Dedicated To

Sandra
Shelley
Scott
Shawn
Staci
Stephanie
and
Shannon

It is my prayer that,
while encouraging others to evangelize,
I will not neglect the salvation
of my own family.

Contents

Prologue

Paul, Kathy
and the Central Church

A vague hollowness had been gnawing at Paul Stewart for a number of months. He was not sure when it started—perhaps it was after he taught the class on Acts the year before—but it was the baptismal clothes which brought it to a head.

They've got to be here, he thought, as a casual search turned into a determined investigation.

Paul had come into the baptistry dressing room to pick up several Bibles for students in his Sunday morning class. It always amazed him that parents would make sure that their children always remembered textbooks for school, but seldom made sure that they took Bibles to study and worship.

He found the Bibles under a stack of towels, picked up several, and idly looked for the white coveralls worn during baptisms. He did not see them on first glance or the second, or the third. Soon he was searching every nook and cranny.

What good would it do to teach someone if we don't have the clothes in which to baptize them? he thought wryly. He checked his wristwatch. *Time for class.*

Paul found the custodian before worship.

"I was looking for the baptismal clothes, but I couldn't find them," he said.

The custodian looked disinterested.

"I'm sure they are there," he replied. "Why? Do we have someone to baptize?"

"No. But what if we did?" Paul said, encouraging the custodian to help him search.

They could not find them.

What would we do? Paul wondered again as minister

George Honeycutt issued the invitation at the end of his standard 35-minute sermon. Then before he could stop the thought: *I hope no one comes forward today; we're not ready.*

After worship he looked again; but the clothing was nowhere to be found.

"Maybe someone's cleaning them," the custodian offered before ambling off, leaving Paul alone.

Paul climbed the steps leading to the baptistry, taking a seat at the top. A film of scum covered the top of the water. Paul dipped his hand into the liquid. It was icy cold!

Lord, what have we come to? It was not the missing baptismal clothing, nor the cold water, nor the film on the water that brought tears to his eyes. It was the soul-searing emptiness that they represented, the hollow Christianity, the mute testimony to a congregation that baptized so few that the accouterments to fulfill that commandment had been misplaced—and not even missed.

As the tears ran down his cheeks, Paul Stewart realized that it was not just a vague hollowness that had been gnawing at him but a lack of spiritual growth. For the first time he wept for souls that are lost and for Christians who are not fulfilling their mission. He wept because, other than his children, he had never converted a soul.

After worship that night, Kathy, his wife, made sandwiches while Paul kindled a blaze in the fireplace. After their three children went to bed, the couple began to re-evaluate their spiritual lives.

To their neighbors and fellow Christians at the Central Church of Christ, the Stewarts are the cream of the crop.

They had met at a Christian college, both Christians since they were 12 years old. Paul's father is an elder, and Paul's mother has taught children's Bible classes as long as he can remember. Kathy's father is a preacher and a Bible professor in a Christian college in a nearby state.

The Stewarts placed membership with the Central congregation the first Sunday after moving into the area. Both teach Bible classes. Paul was quickly asked to serve as a deacon. Lately Kathy has been teaching a women's Bible class on Wednesday evenings.

Every fourth month they host the teen devotional in their home after Sunday night services. Their children have always attended a Christian school.

Ten percent of their budget is returned to the Lord, sometimes more, since they have been married. The Central congregation knows that Paul and Kathy are sick or out of town if they are not at a church service.

The Central church has about 340 members. Sunday morning attendance varies from 290 to 395. Paul and Kathy have often been perplexed as to why the attendance has such a wide variation. Sunday night attendance will average only 150, and on Wednesday nights only 125. But the statistics are not much different than other congregations they have attended.

George Honeycutt is the pulpit minister for the Central congregation. Also, the congregation has a full-time secretary, a part-time educational director, a part-time youth minister and a paid song leader, in addition to the custodian.

The church has five elders and 14 deacons. The contribution is considered to be good, although it has not increased during the past four years. End-of-the-year makeup collections have become necessary to meet its financial committments.

The building of the Central church is six years old with a seating capacity of 850 and an expansion capability to 1,230. The church's property is large enough for it to expand both the building and parking facilities.

The congregation is active in fellowship. One Sunday each quarter, an all-church dinner follows Sunday morning services. Activities also involve youth in a variety of sport and social events. All of the church is encouraged to attend a family camp every summer. At least once a year, the men and women of the congregation plan a separate retreat at a nearby state park. One night a week during the winter is set aside for family games in the activity center.

A food and clothing bank is open by appointment. The senior citizens have a very active group, hosting many parties and trips. Recently a new van was purchased for use by the senior citizens and the youth group.

The congregation has been very receptive to mission work

of all kinds. Visiting missionaries speak frequently, and a larger-than-usual portion of the budget is appropriated for missions.

George Honeycutt, the pulpit minister, has been with the Central congregation for 12 years. He is a serious person, well-respected by other preachers in the area and loved by all of the congregation. Although he does not usually keep regular office hours, everyone in the congregation knows that if they are in the hospital, George will be one of the first to visit them. While George's sermons are usually not more than 35 minutes in length, they seldom contain any illustrations, visual aids or humor.

When George first became Central's preacher, he was fairly active in conducting what were then known as "cottage studies." But it has been at least six or seven years since he has had a personal Bible study with a non-Christian.

A number of people have placed membership with Central during the last few years as it is in a growing part of town. But their Sunday morning attendance has not increased during the last three years.

In an attempt to be evangelistic, the Central church holds annual spring and fall gospel meetings with some of the brotherhood's best preachers invited to speak. Members from other congregations often attend these meetings, but visitors from the community never come. There have been 11 baptisms during the last four years. All but one of those were children of members.

Paul and Kathy reasoned long into the night. They realized that somehow, despite all their busyness, the congregation had missed the mission of Christianity. They understood the subtle dissatisfaction that permeated the congregation, a spiritual restlessness that had also touched their own lives. It was the same dissatisfaction that evidenced itself in the boredom expressed by their children.

Over the past year they had noticed that several of the younger families were absent consistently on Sunday nights. Discreet inquiries found that some were having a separate meeting in their homes while others neglected services to follow worldly pursuits.

"I've compared our congregation to the ones in Acts, and

something is missing," Paul told Kathy as the two prayed in the small hours of the morning.

"I want to ask you a question," he said as he turned to his wife. She noticed that the last embers of the fire gave his face a sad glow.

"Have you ever converted someone?"

The question stunned Kathy. Of course she had.

"Sure."

"Who?"

A long pause.

"The children. You and I both converted them."

"Other than the children. We would expect them to follow our example. We would expect them to become Christians," he said before pressing the point. "But have you ever taught someone the gospel and stood by as they were baptized?"

Another long pause.

"No. I guess not," she finally answered.

"Neither have I."

The two were engrossed in private thoughts.

"I remember how it was when I was baptized," Paul broke the silence. "My heart was so full of excitement, of knowing that I was a sinner who was now saved. I was a 12-year-old child, but I understood sin and salvation."

"Now I'm a grown man. I should have such an understanding that my heart is on fire with the gospel," he continued.

"We go to church. We're good people," he said. "I don't know what happened to us."

Kathy listened, her eyes on the fading embers of the once roaring fire. Gray ash covered the glowing embers, only a bit of color managing to struggle free. She started to get up and prod it, making it cherry red with colorful flames.

The comparison hit her like a thunderbolt.

"Paul," she said, pausing.

"It's like the fire. We've been here all evening long. No one has touched it, and it has slowly died down."

These two concerned Christians knew that somehow they had to rekindle the flame and set their hearts on fire.

Part 1

RECLAIMING EVANGELISM

We Must and We Can Convert the Lost

1 WHATEVER HAPPENED TO EVANGELISM?

Are You Going Doorknocking When Our Yard Needs Mowing?

CHAPTER HIGHLIGHTS

* The Evangelistic State of the Church
* Our Present Strategies Offer Little Hope
* Polar Bears in the Pulpit
* Friendship Evangelism Is Not Enough
* We Are Being Lulled to Sleep

The average member of the church of Christ has heard 4,000 sermons, sung 20,000 songs, participated in 8,000 public prayers . . .

. . . And converted zero sinners.

A sobering and chilling statistic.

How close are you to average?

Now ask yourself:

How many Christians do I know who are actively involved in some kind, any kind, of regular, effective evangelistic outreach?

Perhaps the real question is:

How involved do I honestly want to be?

After reading this statistic you may never be able to hear

another sermon, sing another song or participate in another prayer without a burning desire to rise above the average.

But there is good news about you and the good news:

You do not want to be just average or you would not be participating in this study.

The Evangelistic State of the Church

• The church in Nashville, Tenn. loses 100 more members a year than it gains.

• One large, prestigious congregation during a recent year baptized only four people.

• Another 800-member congregation in that Bible-belt area baptized only eight souls during that same year, and that tiny number of conversions included the 12-year-old children of members!

• A 400-member congregation was recently reminded by the minister that they had not baptized anyone in the last 18 months.

• A large Texas church baptized only 15 people during a recent year which equals about one baptism per full-time staff member.

Are these congregations in Tennessee and Texas much different from churches in California or Alabama or anywhere else in the country? I would imagine that their experience could be very similar to the congregation where you are.

Average.

A lady, probably in her 50s at the time, described an evangelistic campaign she had just completed.

"That was the first time in my life I have been tired for Jesus," she told me, beaming at the memory of long hours in service to the Lord. I wonder how many of us have ever been tired for Jesus?

The status of the church at large today is typified by the husband who was stopped by his wife as he walked out the door one Saturday morning to join fellow Christians who elected to prepare for a special campaign by knocking on doors. Perturbed, his wife exclaimed: "You're going door knocking this morning when our yard needs mowing!"

There is no doubt that some congregations are stagnant. Members need to get out of their air-conditioned, carpeted, stained glass sanctuaries. Church growth has been crippled because we have lost evangelistic contact with people.

"The church is a museum" is a common complaint by Christians and non-Christians, alike, who claim that the divine institution is populated by "dried up" believers.

What would you think of a cafeteria where the employees show up for work at the proper time of the morning, the management lets them in, and then promptly locks the doors and they all spend the day preparing food for each other?

Many of our churches are no longer soul-saving institutions. They are worshiping societies, and their main emphasis is on holding services and social events. Most of our planning is concerned with something that pertains to our assemblies.

What we now have is what is referred to as a "maintenance mentality." This means the attention of the church is focused on itself and its own life. The most important business of the church seems to be meeting to promote the next gathering of its members. The great challenge is keeping the bored and apathetic members coming to the meet-

> The average member of the church of Christ has heard 4,000 sermons, sung 20,000 songs, participated in 8,000 public prayers . . .
> . . . And converted zero sinners.

ings. Our church activities are increasingly inward-focused.

Many congregations are placing more emphasis on buildings, parking lots and carpeting than on redeeming souls. While the church is specifically charged with saving the lost, most of the weekly contribution—sometimes as high as 95 cents out of every dollar—is used to pay expenses for preaching to ourselves or to pay for the building in which we meet to preach to each other. Meanwhile, millions of people who never enter a church building are going unsaved.

Sadly, the general condition of the brotherhood today is very reminiscent of the members of the "lukewarm" church in Laodicea (Revelation 3:14-22).

Only the Parade

Years ago, a small boy who lived in the country heard that a circus was coming to town. In those days, that was really a special treat. He heard also that it only cost a quarter to see.

He worked and saved. Finally the day came for the circus, so he went to town with his quarter. He found a prime spot on the curb, right on Main Street. Perched there, he could not fail to see the circus parade as it entered town on its way to the big tent. He would be so close that he could almost reach out and touch the clowns and the wild animals.

After working and saving his money and waiting breathlessly on the street, at last he saw the circus parade come blaring down Main Street, much to his joyful anticipation. It was more than he had imagined: ponderous elephants, roaring tigers in their cages, acrobats and clowns. It all passed right in front of him, so close that it took his breath away.

As the parade neared its end, the appreciative little boy, who had dreamed and worked for this wondrous moment, ran out into the street, where he handed his quarter to one of the startled circus clowns. Without a word, the little boy turned and skipped happily home, thinking he had seen the circus!

We could all benefit from this slogan about priorities:

"The main thing is to keep the main thing the main thing."

The point is obvious. We have faithfully attended services, preached to each other within the confines of the four walls of our buildings, even given our money, and then gone home thinking we have been evangelistic. We have been satisfied with just seeing the parade.

Tickets for one Broadway play had to be purchased months in advance. One couple even planned their entire vacation around the availability of tickets.

But, to their surprise, they discovered an empty seat next to them when they arrived for the show. It was the only vacant seat in the theater.

"This is amazing," the man said to a woman seated across from the empty seat. "We had to buy our tickets eight months in advance, and we get here and find an empty seat."

The woman replied, "Well, that seat belongs to me, too."

"It was my husband's seat," she continued with a shrug. "He died!"

The man said, "I'm terribly sorry. But couldn't you have invited a friend to come with you?"

She thought about it a second before answering. "No, I couldn't do that; they are all at his funeral!"

Now that is a woman who has clear priorities!

Are our priorities as Christians as turned around as hers?

God never intended for Christianity to be church-building centered. The message from God in the New Testament is that He intends for us to go to the lost (Matthew 28:19, 20; Acts 26:16-18; Romans 1:14,15; 2 Timothy 2:2). Instead, our usual evangelistic program involves having a nice building and nice services to which the lost can come. And if they don't come, they are not reached.

If our church-building evangelism method could win America, it would already have done so. If we were to di-agram how our present methods anticipate membership through a "come-to-us" mentality, it would look like this:

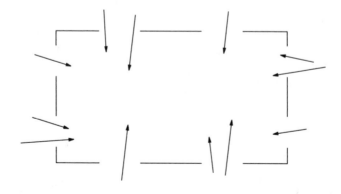

It is ironic when one stops to think about it. In an age when facilities for rapid communication of the Gospel are available to the church as never before, we are actually accomplishing less in winning the world for God than before the invention of the horseless carriage.[1]

Our present attitude toward evangelism is sometimes like the football player asked by his coach what he would do if their team had the ball on the opponents' one-yard line and had only one play in which to make a touchdown. He replied that he would move to the end of the bench where he could get a better view of what was going on down there!

It has been said that the church of the 20th century resembles a professional football game. Seventy thousand spectators desperately in need of exercise watch 22 men on the field who are desperately in need of rest.

Our Present Strategies Offer Little Hope

Most evangelism methods the church is using today are essentially ineffective. To substantiate that statement all we have to do is look at what is being accomplished.

Church sociologist Win Arn says that at least 75 percent of American churches have plateaued or are experiencing a decline in membership. Many of our congregations have been the same size for years. They will probably be that same size for years to come. Most of the churches that are numerically growing are growing only because their church building is located in a booming suburb, and people are placing membership from other congregations.

Membership figures among churches of Christ reflect these discouraging statistics:

• 89 percent of our congregations have fewer than 200 members

• 73 percent of our congregations have fewer than 100 members

• 50 percent of our congregations have fewer than 50 members

If we project the non-growth trends of the last few years into the future, it seems obvious that our present strategies offer little hope of significantly impacting our culture and winning multitudes to the Lord.

Polar Bears in the Pulpit

Even ministers are not providing leadership for evangelism. How many preachers do you know who are actively holding any kind of evangelistic, interpersonal Bible studies?

Yet the example of the ministers and elders usually sets the pace for the congregation. A church will seldom have a greater soul-winning vision than that inspired by the preacher!

Within the last few years, one concerned sister has written to two different ministers in other cities about people in their vicinity she believed they could help save. In both instances, she knew the people involved and offered information that would gain the ministers an open door. In both cases, she never received a reply, and no contact with those people was ever made.

> How many Christians do I know who are actively involved in some kind, any kind, of regular, effective evangelistic outreach?

Someone said that if there are icebergs in the pew, it is because there is a polar bear in the pulpit. A preacher was recently waiting to preach and noticed a fire extinguisher on the side of the pulpit. He thought this was very strange. But the more he thought about it, the more appropriate it seemed, because if a fire is going to start anywhere it is likely to start in the pulpit. And if it does not start there, it probably won't start.

Every church should be experiencing regular baptisms. If there are no baptisms over an extended period of time, this means that not even the preacher is active in trying to convert the lost.

A Passionate Priority

A minister needs to have strong personal convictions in this matter. Evangelism must be a personal priority. If he does not live it, he cannot preach it with conviction. And if it is not preached, it will not be accomplished.

Evangelism must become a passionate priority. Paul explained his own motivation when he said, "Christ's love compels us" (2 Corinthians 5:14).

Friendship Evangelism Is Not Enough

If you were to ask ministers about their approach to evangelism, many of them would answer that they believe in "friendship evangelism." Friendship evangelism, as practiced in this context, is essentially cultivating a friendship with an unbeliever. The intent is that your friends will notice your better life and eventually come to you for answers to solve their problems and to also enjoy a fulfilled life. This is not the textbook definition of friendship evangelism, but it is what is being practiced by its proponents.

First Peter 2:12 does teach that the example of the Christian life is a powerful example for the unbeliever and will definitely have an impact on his life:

> Live such good lives among the pagans that, though they accuse you of doing wrong, they may see your good deeds and glorify God on the day he visits us.

First Peter 3:1,2 also teaches this principle as an effective means for wives to convert nonbelieving husbands:

> Wives, in the same way be submissive to your husbands so that, if any of them do not believe the word, they may be won over without talk by the behavior of their wives, when they see the purity and reverence of your lives.

But these passages must be combined with the Bible emphasis on the necessity to verbally express our faith. In Acts 8:21, the Ethiopian asks Philip, "'How can I,' he said, 'unless someone explains it to me?'" We must talk about our faith. Another very clear illustration of this principle is Paul's statement in Philemon 6: "I pray that you may be active in sharing your faith."

Many conversions in Acts were the result of someone verbally explaining God's will. When the angel released the apostles from public jail in Acts 5:20, they were told: "'Go, stand in the temple courts," he said, "and *tell* the people the full message of this new life.'" The blind Saul of Tarsus was commanded, "'Now get up and go into the city, and you will be *told* what you must do.'"

Another example of this principle is when Priscilla and Aquilla heard Apollos preaching an incomplete gospel. Acts 18:26 says, "When Priscilla and Aquilla heard him, they invited him to their house and *explained* to him the way of God more adequately." Successful evangelism requires this New Testament kind of boldness!

While friendship evangelism is a necessary part of the Christian life, it is not aggressive enough to convert the world. What if my friends do not notice my better life and ask for directions to Jesus? In God's scheme of motivation, friendship helps soften people so they will be receptive to the Word, but it is not the stopping point.

> Many of our churches are no longer soul-saving institutions. They are worshipping societies, and their main emphasis is on holding services and social events.

The danger is that Christians often hide behind this approach. They seek to justify inactivity with the excuse that their relationship with someone is not strong enough yet to mention the Gospel. Friendship evangelism is too often used as an excuse to justify a lethargic attitude toward the lost.

Herb Miller writes:

> . . . distorted interpretation of Matthew 5:14-16 says that if you live an exemplary Christian life, people will see your good works

11

and want to become Christians, themselves. Close scrutiny reveals that this is the religious version of an old secular saying: "If you build a better mousetrap the world will beat a path to your door." That was never completely true of mousetraps, and it is not true of Christianity. A Christian's life-style rarely by itself produces new Christians. Christianity is communicable, but is seldom caught visually.[2]

We Are Being Lulled to Sleep

A long time friend and brother in Christ has just left the church. He was a full-time employee of the church at the time he left.

Not long after he left, I had lunch with him. He told me about a telephone conversation with the former pulpit minister of that church. I asked him what the minister had said to him about his decision to leave the church. He said that they had chatted for 30-45 minutes, and not one word was said about it.

The same thing happened when he had lunch with another former staff associate. Since he left not one word had been said, not one visit had been made by any of the ministers, elders, deacons or members of that church in an effort to convict him of his error! And that congregation has several thousand members. That just shouts that it really did not bother his brethren that a former minister is now lost.

> Even ministers are not providing leadership for evangelism. How many preachers do you know who are actively holding any kind of evangelistic, interpersonal Bible studies?

Our problem is that we have become spiritually lethargic. We are like a car stuck in a snowdrift—the wheels are spinning and the motor is racing, but there is no forward movement. Congregations have full calendars with lots of programs and activities but no forward direction that will keep the main thing the main thing—growth.

We have become indifferent. It doesn't really matter to us that we are not growing. People are lost, and we are evangelistically inactive.

Immediately after the period of the New Testament, many of those who became Christians were persecuted because of their faith. They were jailed, beaten, killed in arenas for entertainment, and persecuted in many other ways.

I suspect the Devil thought that the church would go out of existence if people knew that by being members of it, they would be persecuted or perhaps even killed. But it didn't work. Historians tell us that when a Christian's blood stained the ground, four more Christians arose out of that blood. Many pagans were converted when they saw that Christian martyrs had something for which they were willing to die.

Perhaps the Devil learned a lesson from that. Today he is not persecuting us; he is lulling us to sleep. That is his method for destroying the church in our generation. The character of the church is tested in times of comfort and affluence as well as in times of crisis and persecution. James Thompson illustrates this in *The Church in Exile:*

> We hear of the vitality of the faith in distant places under the worst conditions imaginable. Civil wars, government oppression, and economic disaster cannot stop the growth of Christianity in some parts of the Third World. In our own country, however, we have watched as congregations have grown older and smaller.[3]

I suspect that we are not really convinced that most people are lost today. Many Christians act as if Heaven and Hell are just fantasies someone made up, like Santa Claus and the tooth fairy.

It appears that we have chosen to isolate ourselves and enjoy our exclusive private "church clubs." If this is not correct, what would have to be different to make it so?

It seems clear that few Christians care about the lost. If we do care, why is so little being done to fulfill the mission of the church and save the lost?

When is the last time you tried to teach someone? When is the last time you prayed in agony for the Lord to lead you to some lost soul that you could help teach?

Evangelism in most congregations of the church of Christ today is not a priority! Interpersonal evangelism is almost non-existent. The baptisms we are having are coming through "biological evangelism," the children of Christians.

We are no longer fishers of men. We are keepers of the aquarium and what we call growing is often just swiping fish from each other's bowl.

Most of us are not concerned enough about the lost to even pray about them. When was the last time you heard someone in a church service pray fervently for the lost and for the attitude of the congregation to become more evangelistic?

Our problem is not that people won't listen to the gospel, our problem is that we are not talking to them about it.

If you are beginning to feel a little uncomfortable by now, please keep reading just a little longer. In the final analysis, I believe you will find this book positive and constructive, not negative. It is my prayer that, through this study, you find encouragement and some answers. I believe that in our hearts most of us really do want to grow. Nothing is more exciting than seeing someone we have taught baptized, and I think that many people in the church want to reach the lost but lack the practical leadership to achieve that.

As you read the chapters to come, rethink your personal ministry and how you and the church you are a part of can become more effective at reaching the lost. This is an enormously difficult yet potentially productive and satisfying challenge.

Sneak Preview

Because people are lost and God demands that they be taught, soul-winning needs to be the supreme goal in our lives and the top priority in each of our congregations. We have in our possession the greatest gift available to mankind—the greatest news ever announced—and because there is an urgency attached to it, it must be taught. We will talk about that in the next chapter.

Discussion Starters

The typical class length may not allow time for both the "Discussion Starters" and "Response to This Chapter." Use whatever portion best suits the personality of your class.

1. To help you to relate these concepts to your congregation, find answers to the questions below.
   A. How many members did your congregation have five years ago?
   B. How many have been baptized in the last five years?
   C. How many of those who have been baptized were members' children?
   D. How many were baptized last year?
   E. What percentage of your budget is spent on preaching to the congregation or for the building in which the preaching occurs?
2. Who are the "lost?" Define this carefully, as it is crucial to your motivation.
3. Do you believe you are concerned about the lost? What are you doing to express that concern?
4. Describe how your congregation would be different if new people were being baptized weekly.
5. What are the priorities in your congregation? How do you know? Are they in the correct order?
6. Why is it so easy—almost natural—for Christians today to turn into spectators rather than participants?
7. How would you relate friendship to evangelism?
8. Do you agree that our Christianity is being stifled by comfort and affluence? If you agree, relate how it is affecting you personally.
9. Are methods part of our problem in winning the minds and souls of men?
10. Guilt is not a comfortable emotion, but does it ever serve a good purpose?

RESPONSE TO THIS CHAPTER

1. For me, the most meaningful part of chapter one is

   _____

   _____

   Why?

   _____

2. One thing in chapter one I do not understand is

   _____

   _____

3. One thing I do not agree with in this chapter is

   _____

   _____

   Why?

   _____

4. The one point in this chapter I wish our group could discuss further is

   _____

   _____

5. Other reactions I have to this chapter are

   _____

   _____

MY PERSONAL COMMITMENT

1. I will try to be available to any new idea God may want to give me during the course.
2. I will be available to any member of this group for prayer, friendship and support in these sessions.
3. I will give the group meetings social priority—that is, try to attend all meetings.
4. I will do my best to read the next chapter in the student book before each session.

Signed: _____

Date: _____

Notes

1. Robert E. Coleman, *The Master Plan of Evangelism* (Old Tappan, N.J.: Fleming H. Revell, 1987), p. 36.
2. Herb Miller, *How to Build A Magnetic Church* (Nashville: Abingdon Press, 1987), p. 29.
3. James Thompson, *The Church in Exile* (Abilene, Texas: ACU Press, 1990), p. 46.

2 LIFE'S MOST IMPORTANT ACHIEVEMENT

Not A Boll of Cotton in the Whole Field

CHAPTER HIGHLIGHTS

* The Most Important Thing in the World Is to Save A Soul
* Saving the Lost Was First in the Priorities of Jesus
* God's Plan for Evangelism Is Revealed through Paul's Example
* Every Christian Was Won to Win Others
* Why Does the Church Exist? What Are Its Priorities?
* We Are in the People Business

Several years ago, my family was camping in the mountains of Colorado. We had arrived there late in the afternoon, and we picked out a nice spot close to a beautiful river. While I was attending to the chores of setting up and organizing our camp, the children went off to play.

As the sun began to set, we started rounding up the children and hustling them back into our campground before it got completely dark. Our four-year-old son, Scott, was missing. The river was making so much noise that my calls were drowned out, and its roar was a constant reminder of danger.

Panic began to build. Where was he? Had he wandered out of the campground? Had he wandered up or down the river? The last time I saw him, he was playing at the edge of the water with a little boat he had made.

By now you could barely distinguish the camp as the rays of the setting sun were further blocked by the forest. A chilling reality gripped me. I only had a few minutes before darkness made my search nearly impossible.

What should I do?

First, I want to tell you some of the things I did not do.

I did not organize any classes on how to find lost children.

I did not hold any rallies to enlist volunteers to help me.

I did not wait until someone came along who was better qualified than I to search. I did not fail to do anything for fear of doing the wrong thing.

Now, I want to tell you what I did do. I acted immediately. I ran around the campground. I dashed up and down the river. I called Scott's name, in spite of the roaring river. I searched the churning waters. I stopped total strangers to describe him, and they joined in the search.

> "If man has a soul, and he has, and if that soul can be won or lost for eternity, and it can, then the most important thing in the world is to bring a man to Jesus Christ."

Nothing else mattered for that period of time. Finding him was my top priority.

After running all over the campground and up and down the river, I still could not find him. Not knowing what else to do, I decided to go back to camp to figure out what to do next. Scott and I arrived at the same time. He was walking nonchalantly into our campground, oblivious to everything; I was still on a dead run.

An older preacher once said, "If man has a soul, and he has, and if that soul can be won or lost for eternity, and it can, then the most important thing in the world is to bring a man to Jesus Christ."

Is he right?

A young man entering medical school in Africa had achieved a lifetime dream. As a young lad, Apollo watched with growing horror as three out of every four babies born in his village died before they turned four years old. Just by growing into young adulthood, Apollo had already beaten tremendous odds. When he enrolled in medical school, he joined another elite corps, since only one in a million black Africans ever have the opporunity to become a medical doctor.

However, Apollo was converted while he was in medical school. Not long after his conversion he announced he was giving up his medical studies. His friends and professors were astounded. But to Apollo it was simple. His mother and father, his brothers and sisters and all his friends would die eternally without Jesus Christ. Saving their souls was more important than saving their bodies. This dedicated man has established 17 congregations in Africa.

Maintain the Institution or Save Souls

Saving the lost was Jesus Christ's first priority. To the people critical of His association with Zacchaeus, Jesus explained His interest by saying, "For the Son of Man came to seek and to save what was lost" (Luke 19:10).

In John 4, the disciples returned from a trip into a village to get something to eat. Jesus had just concluded His conversation with the Samaritan woman at the well. He was so excited at the prospect of saving a soul that food had lost its appeal. When the disciples pressed Him, He explained His lack of hunger: "I have food to eat that you know nothing about."

He continued, "My food . . . is to do the will of Him who sent me and to finish His work" (John 4:32, 34). Being able to do the will of God was so important to Jesus that it transcended the need for food.

Jesus not only practiced this priority; He also taught it. This is what He was doing when teaching the disciples about the vine and the branches:

> He cuts off every branch in me that bears no fruit, while every branch that does bear fruit he trims clean so that it will be even more fruitful (John 15:2).

God is not pleased with fruitless branches. He wants branches that produce fruit. Barren branches are an encumberance, and always a hindrance, to the work of the Lord. Christ once demonstrated his displeasure with fruitlessness when, to the astonishment of His apostles, He cursed a barren fig tree (Matthew 21:18,19).

Christ further explained in John 15 that the purpose of both the vine (Himself) and the branches (believers in Him) is to bear fruit. Any branch that does not produce is to be cut off—it is worthless. Any branch attached to the vine is meant to produce. Even the branches that do produce are pruned so that they might yield even more fruit (John 15:2). It is very clear from this passage that the life-sustaining power of the vine is not going to be endlessly supplied to unfruitful branches.

Jesus applied this illustration to His disciples, an application as valid today as it was then. As surely as they depended on Him for life, even so they had to bear His fruit (John 15:5, 8). A barren Christian is a contradiction.

It is interesting, too, that every time fruitbearing is mentioned in this passage, the Greek word is in the present tense, which means that it is a continuing state—something that keeps on reproducing.[1]

When I was a young boy growing up on an Arkansas farm, one year my folks planted a new patch of ground in cotton. Cotton stalks are usually about knee-high, but these soon towered as tall as my head. They were big and bushy, beautiful and green, a sight to bring joy to the heart of any farmer—until he inspected his crop. Dad discovered that there was not a boll of cotton in the whole field. As far as he was concerned, that field of beautiful cotton stalks was worthless; he would have no harvest that year.

What is most important in your congregation: the building? proper teaching? programs? What about people? A study of Jesus and His ministry reveals a strong sensitivity to people. His concern for the welfare of people made Him yearn for them to be saved. This is stressed in Matthew 9:36-38.

> When he saw the crowds, he had compassion on them, because they were harassed and helpless, like sheep without a shepherd. Then he said to his disciples, "The harvest is plentiful but the workers are few. Ask the Lord of the harvest, therefore, to send out workers into his harvest field."

His Converts Converted Others

When talking with the Samaritan woman, Christ became so excited at the opportunity to save a soul that He lost interest in food. The woman left her water pot at the well and went back to tell her neighbors about His astonishing knowledge.

> Many of the Samaritans from that town believed in him because of the woman's testimony, "He told me everything I ever did" . . . And because of his words many more became believers (John 4:39, 41).

The reason some of us do not bring the lost to Jesus is not because of a lack of knowledge or a lack of training. Rather, it is because we have not become excited at hearing the Word, like the Samaritan woman.

Pass It On!

God's plan for evangelism is also revealed through the example of Paul's preaching. The principle is succintly given by Paul in 2 Timothy 2:2:

> And the things you have heard me say in the presence of many witnesses entrust to reliable men who will also be qualified to teach others.

After Paul made new disciples, he continued to teach them God's Word in order to strengthen them as Christians.

They then did the same thing for others that he had done for them.

Here is the model for this principle:

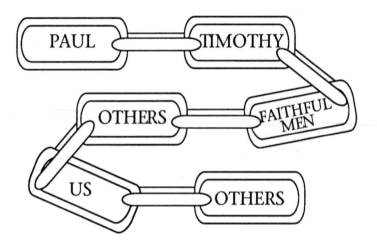

And this is to go on . . . and on . . . and on . . . and on . . . until Jesus comes!

Disciple-Making Our No. 1 Priority

In the city of Gourd Neck, there are two congregations, Northside and Southside. They are about the same size in membership. Both are made up of middle-class people, and both are considering taking on a financial challenge.

At Northside, the evangelism committee has discovered the enormous potential that the church has for reaching the unsaved in its immediate area. But the preacher is over-worked, and the evangelism committee needs some professional guidance and leadership. They have recommended that the congregation hire a minister of evangelism.

The annual cost for such a worker would be $40,000. This person would train and equip members of the church to share their faith more effectively. He would also be in charge of developing an outreach mentality in the congregation.

Across town, the members at Southside are faced with a $40,000 challenge as well. The parking lot is in bad need of resurfacing, and the carpet in the auditorium is wearing thin in many places. The building and grounds committee has recommended to the congregation that they begin a fund-raising activity to collect $40,000 to resurface the parking lot and recarpet the auditorium as soon as possible.

To a large degree, the success of the proposals at Northside and Southside will be based on the **mission or maintenance mentality** of the congregations. In most congregations, the probability of resurfacing and recarpeting is much greater than the probability of hiring an evangelist because many have lost the vision for their mission. They have settled into a maintenance mentality. For many, maintaining the institution is the mission of the church. But saving souls, not maintaining the institution, is the only gospel-inspired mission of the church.

Why does the church exist? What are its priorities? What has God called the church to be and to do?

The example of Jesus and those He converted, would teach us that the making of new disciples (Matthew 28:18-20) is the supreme business of life and the first priority in each congregation. That was the chief business of Jesus, it was the chief business of Paul, it was the chief business of those early Christians in the book of Acts, and it should be the chief business of contemporary Christians, as well.

God has to use you and me to get His message to the world. The only way the love of Jesus will ever be known by the lost is through us. This is the way God designed it to be. There are myriads of other ways the message could have been disseminated, but God choose the method of *each one teach one,* and His goal can only be accomplished through active believers. This is the method Jesus authorized in the Great Commission.

The most effective messengers of the Word are just regular Christians—not the paid ministerial staff. The hard truth is that many people are uncomfortable in a Biblical discussion with a preacher. Sometimes they are intimidated by the minister's vast knowledge of the Bible. For this reason, the world will never be reached just by preachers. The New Testament is clear that even those who are not preachers or evangelists are still ministers (2 Corinthians 3:6; 5:20; 6:1; 1 Peter 4:11).

Fanning the Flame

Every Christian was saved to save others through Jesus Christ. World evangelism is not a minor endeavor but the major enterprise of the church.

I read once of some missionaries who offered themselves as slaves in order to get into China to do mission work. Someone has said that "the church exists by evangelism as fire exists by burning." In every church there is a sleeping power that, if fanned into flame, could do wonders for God.

How wonderful it would be if every Christian today was not just a convert, but a converter. If God so loved the world that He gave His Son, is it too much to ask that the church of Christ so love the world that it give itself to the fulfillment of the Great Commision, which is man's only hope for eternity. Maybe Christians are not making converts because we are not yet converted!

We're in the people business because God is in the people business. The point of church growth is not numbers, but numbers of people.

The harvest of souls is thrilling. If you have never had the experience of being a part of bringing a soul to Jesus, you have missed one of the most precious experiences of life.

The Urgency

Making evangelism even more urgent for us is the fact that there are more unsaved people today than a year ago. In the early 1990s, the population of the United States was 247.1 million. Approximately 10,731 babies are born each day, but only 5,895 people die daily, a net gain of around 5,000 people every day. And, there is a net gain in world population of 244,427 every 24 hours.

Hoarding the Good News

In 2 Kings 7:3-9 is a story that illustrates an important evangelism principle. The story begins as Samaria is under siege, and because of this they have no food.

> Now there were four men with leprosy at the entrance of the city gate. They said to each other, "Why stay here until we die? If we say, 'We'll go into the city'—the famine is there, and we will die. And if we stay here, we will die. So let's go over to the camp of the Arameans and surrender. If they spare us, we live, if they kill us, then we die."
> At dusk they got up and went to the camp of the Arameans. When they reached the edge of the camp, not a man was there, for the Lord had caused the Arameans to hear the sound of chariots and horses and a great army, so that they said to one another, "Look, the king of Israel has hired the Hittite and Egyptian kings to attack us!" So they got up and fled in the dusk and abandoned their tents and their horses and donkeys. They left the camp as it was and ran for their lives.
> The men who had leprosy reached the edge of the camp and entered one of the tents. They ate and drank, and carried away silver, gold and clothes, and went off and hid them. They returned and entered another tent and took some things from it and hid them also.
> Then they said to each other. "We're not doing right. This is a day of good news and we are keeping it to ourselves. If we wait until daylight, punishment will overtake us. Let's go at once and report this to the royal palace."

These lepers came to the conclusion their selfishness was wrong. When we realize that withholding the good news of salvation is selfish and wrong, evangelism will really accelerate.

The Great Omission

The conclusion of all of this is that the Great Commission is not an optional command. The Great Commission is a personal, individual command to every child of God to go into his own personal world and try to convert every person who will listen. For many, however, the Great Commission has become the great omission.

Jesus uses the lives and lips of dedicated disciples. The New Testament places the responsibility for evangelism on every individual Christian. No one can fulfill my responsibility to teach the lost anymore than he could be baptized for me or observe the Lord's Supper for me. These are responsibilities that cannot be delegated just because we have something else we would prefer to do.

Very few men or women will discover the plan of salvation on their own. It is up to Christians to lead them to the Way, just as Philip had to lead the treasurer from Ethiopia (Acts 8).

> The Great Commission is a personal, individual command to every child of God to go into his own personal world and try to convert every person who will listen.

Another native preacher in Africa is a blind man named Godwin McGwakwa. Two missionaries heard that the church had been established in a certain village. They went there and asked if this was so. They met the brethren and inquired of them who had started the church there. "Why, the blind man did," they replied.

He had come to preach and had baptized 43 in that village. They said that he would walk as much as 80 miles through the African jungle to reach villages to preach. They reported that he was known to have the Bible read to him all night long.

Men like Apollo and Godwin are illustrations of the fruits of Paul's principle of evangelism:

> And the things you have heard me say in the presence of many witnesses entrust to reliable men who will also be qualified to teach others (2 Timothy 2:2).

Sneak Preview

In the next chapter, we will explore the confidence God wants all of His people to have so that we can grow and convert the lost.

On the basis of the thoughts in this chapter, let's look at how we can improve.

Discussion Starters

1. What do you feel, based on their actions, is the most important goal of your congregation?
2. Have you ever been directly responsible for helping someone become a Christian? If so, describe how you felt about it.
3. Why do you think more of us haven't been involved in leading someone to Christ?
4. How many in the class are Christians because someone helped them to Jesus?
5. Explain Jesus' lack of hunger in John 4:32, 34? Are we like Him in this area?
6. Do you have any comments to make about the importance of the plans of the Northside and Southside churches?
7. What was it that made the author panic and rush to find his son? Can you make any applications to evangelism from this story?
8. What does the statement "the church exists by evangelism as fire exists by burning" mean?

RESPONSE TO THIS CHAPTER

1. For me, the most meaningful part of chapter two is

   _____

   _____

   Why?

   _____

2. One thing in chapter two I do not understand is

   _____

   _____

3. One thing I do not agree with in this chapter is

   _____

   _____

   Why?

   _____

4. The one point in this chapter I wish our group could discuss further is

   _____

   _____

5. Other reactions I have to this chapter are

   _____

   _____

NOTES

1. Robert E. Coleman, *The Master Plan of Evangelism* (Old Tappan, NJ: Fleming H. Revell, 1987), p. 107.

3 YOUR CONGREGATION CAN GROW

How Many Kernels Are On An Ear of Corn?

CHAPTER HIGHLIGHTS

* We Can Accomplish Whatever We Want
* Reversing Our Thinking Patterns
* God's Power Is Greater than Any Obstacle
* God's Word Is Powerful Enough to Accomplish Whatever Needs to Be Done

Few people have the courage of their convictions.

While living in Denver, I attended a workshop in a distant state. Much to my surprise, I came across a family that I had known in Denver. I was even more astonished when they revealed they had just moved to the city in which the host congregation was located.

Why had they left their home in Denver? They had visited this congregation while on vacation and were impressed. They had always wanted to be a part of a dynamic, growing group of Christians, so they left their home to move to the new city.

33

I have often thought of that family's unique action. Many of us would like to be part of a great church, but we do not want to move across the country to do so. Since many of us want to be members of a great church like that one, but we don't want to move, why don't we make great churches out of the one where we are now?

Getting Out of God's Way

Do you realize that we can accomplish whatever great things we want to in the Lord's work? The emphasis in Biblical evangelism is not on what we can do but on what God can achieve through us. The "main thing" in Christian service is to let God effectively implement the Great Commission by using us. Sometimes, though, we frustrate God with a lukewarm attitude that gets in the way of His work and of His plans.

The challenge is for us to cooperate with God's intentions for His church. We can achieve whatever great goals the Lord wants us to accomplish! After all, thirteen men once evangelized the whole world simply by telling the Good News of salvation, and often that was to people who had never heard of the Word of God.

Conversions recorded in the book of Acts were not due to a super effective, charismatic preacher but because of the Word they preached. Jesus knew the power of the Word when He told His apostles, "The harvest is plentiful but the workers are few. Ask the Lord of the harvest, therefore, to send out workers into his harvest field" (Matthew 9:37,38). Workers are being sought to harvest the crop that the Lord of the harvest has already grown!

The terminology used in Acts 12:24 is "But the word of God continued to increase and spread." The emphasis is not on the good job the workers are doing. It is on the Word of God. The Bible is teaching us here that the Word of God generates the conversions. This principle is again illustrated in 1 Corinthians 3:6 when Paul said, "I planted the seed, Apollos watered it, but God made it grow."

The point is further emphasized by Paul in 2 Corinthians 9:10,

Now he who supplies seed to the sower and bread for food will also supply and increase your store of seed and will enlarge the harvest of your righteousness.

Paul teaches that the God who supplies seed and makes our daily bread will help you evangelize in that same manner. A scientist could never make a bushel of seeds in the laboratory. A complex mixture of microscopic ingredients goes into creating a single seed so that it will germinate in life-giving soil, draw strength from moisture, thrust a frail stem into life-sustaining sunlight, and then draw sustenance from soil, water and sun so that it grows into a single stalk that yields numerous seeds at harvest.

> Do you realize that God can make churches grow and that He can make it possible for us to reach and baptize many?

God has set in motion all these continuing laws of nature. If we follow them, we will reap the bounty that fills our tables and sustains our lives. Mankind may bake a loaf of bread, but only God's laws can cause the seed to grow.

The same simple principle works in conversion. We sow the seeds in the hearts of the lost and God provides the harvest.

The fact that God will work through us is again emphasized by Paul in two other passages:

Now to him who is able to do immeasurably more than all we ask or imagine, **according to his power that is at work within us** (Ephesians 3:20).

We proclaim him, admonishing and teaching everyone with all wisdom, so that we may present everyone perfect in Christ. To this end I labor, struggling, with all his energy, **which so powerfully works in me** (Colossians 1:28,29).

Your Congregation Can Grow

A marvelous and challenging thought for those of us in congregations that are not currently fulfilling the Great Commission is that growth is possible. The only way that growth would not be possible is if God has asked us to accomplish something impossible. Remember, He never asked us to create the seed—just harvest the crop.

The Bible not only commands us to grow but assures us that we can. We do not have to accept the status quo in a non-growing, nonevangelizing congregation. We can change things. In most cases, all we have to do is reverse our thinking pattern.

> **The Bible not only commands us to grow but assures us that we can . . . We can change things. In most cases, all we have to do is reverse our thinking pattern.**

The kind of thinking that has hindered growth is like that of the lady who went to the big city for the first time and checked into a large, prestigious hotel. The bellhop picked up her suitcase. She followed him across the lobby into a room. As the door shut, she looked around and began to complain, "This room is so small you can hardly turn around, there isn't any furniture in it, and there isn't even a bathroom."

"Madam," he said patiently, "This isn't your room. This is the elevator."

You Can Make a Difference

God has asked us to go and preach His Word. A congregation that follows this command cannot help but grow.

Perhaps you are in a congregation that has not been growing, which is very discouraging. Do you realize that God can make churches grow and that He can make it possible to reach and baptize many? The way to allow Him to do this in our congregations is to give Him the opportunity to work through us. The only way this will not work is if we are not interested in God working through us to convert lost people or because we are not concerned enough about their being lost to do anything about it.

Levis, Amway and Mickey Mouse

When I look at the Coca-Cola company, I am convinced the church could grow fantastically. This secular company has put a bottle of Coke in virtually every hand in the world. If they can do it with a soft drink, surely we can do it with the Gospel, particularly with God on our side.

The corporations of the world are not having any trouble getting their message to everyone. I see Levi jeans and Crest toothpaste and Amway doing it. Is there anyone out there who does not recognize Mickey Mouse or who has never heard of Disneyland or Disney World?

Hardly a week passes without the mail containing an application for a credit card from a bank in Chicago or Iowa or a plea from American Express to move up to the gold card.

Sales people of all sorts keep the telephones buzzing with offers of aluminium siding, family portraits or burial plots. Politicians regularly reach out to every voter in their precincts by telephone or mail. Everything is being brought to the attention of modern man *except* what he needs most—the gospel.

The secular world can sell anything. Pet rocks and hula hoops had their moments in the spotlight. Products that are absolutely useless are sold by the millions. If people can market those kinds of things, Christians should be able to market the gospel.

There is no obstacle to reaching and converting the lost that won't crumble in the presence of God's power. The gospel is the power of God unto salvation.

The only thing that stands in the way of converting the lost is you and me. Nothing else is strong enough to impede the progress of the gospel.

Congregations that have reached a numerical plateau or, worse, decline have rediscovered the thrill of growth through the reapplication of Biblical principles.

Look in Your Hand

We need to learn to be confident in the Lord. The Lord will take care of the battles and win the victories for us. One of the most powerful lessons God ever taught is contained in the Old Testament when a trembling, fearful Moses stood in the presence of the Creator of the world at the burning bush in Exodus 4. When God asked Moses, "What is that in your hand?" the Lord began to teach us a lesson through Moses.

Moses learned a valuable lesson that echos through the ages to us: **A person becomes powerful when he turns himself over to the Lord.**

Moses at that time was 80 years old. His only work experience was in leading sheep. He had a stammering voice and a lack of self-confidence. But when he submitted to God and let God work through him, he became one of the world's great leaders.

A shepherd's staff in Moses' hand became the force that divided the Red Sea and delivered a mighty nation from 430 years of slavery because God was working through him. Little sticks in the hands of weak men and women become mighty powers in the hand of God.

> There is no obstacle to reaching and converting the lost that won't crumble in the presence of God's power.

This same lesson is illustrated again and again throughout the Bible. Young David defeated towering Goliath in 1 Samuel 17. When God chose Gideon to deliver Israel from the Midianites, Gideon wondered, "How can I save Israel? My clan is the weakest in Manasseh, and I am the least in my family" (Judges 6:15).

Does that sound familar? The obstacles that need to be overcome to talk to someone about Christ leave many Christians feeling just like Gideon or Moses.

But the solution is the same today as it was those many years ago. "The Lord answered, 'I will be with you, and you will strike down the Midianites as if they were but one man'" (Judges 6:16).

I can just hear Peter's thoughts when Jesus told him to hang up his fishing net and become a "fisher of men."

"I can't teach and convert people! I've never spoken before a crowd in my life!"

Yet his preaching of the gospel changed the course of the

world on the day of Pentecost as Christ's prophecy was fulfilled that Peter would open the Kingdom of Heaven. He became powerful when he accepted the direction of the Lord.

None of the apostles had any outstanding traits that identified them as leadership material. They were perceived as ignorant Galilean fishermen—day laborers, we would say. But when they allowed God to work through them, they became as powerful as Moses, David or Gideon.

Don't Whittle God's Stick

A Christian's confidence in his or her ability to help a congregation grow ought to soar every time he realizes the dynamic reality that a few words from his mouth has to lead a soul to salvation. It does not matter if our education is basic, or that our speech patterns reflect our geographic birthplace, or even if the words come stammering out of our mouths. It is not an individual that convicts a man's heart; it is God's Word. As Moses, David and Gideon learned, more depends on the consecrated hand than the weapon in the hand.

This was a lesson that one minister took years to learn as he toiled in the harvest fields, trying to convert people through home Bible studies. Before he left his home, he would be so nervous that his churning stomach would only allow him to sample dinner. When he returned after several hours, he would flop into a chair, a victim of nervous exhaustion. He believed that the conversion and ultimate salvation of the people with whom he was studying depended on how well he could present the gospel and how well he could answer any objections to the Bible's teachings.

Unknowingly, this earnest young preacher had shouldered a responsibility that was not his. By believing that his students' conversion depended solely on his ability to do a good job, he was whittling on God's end of the stick.

The turning point came during a Bible study with a young man who was reared in the Roman Catholic Church. With great detail, the minister presented the New Testament concept of the church and the way God authorized worship in contrast to the practices that the student had been taught in the Catholic faith. As the study came to a conclusion, it was time for the student to make a decision.

"I have heard what you have had to say," he told the young minister. "I would like to go to the priest and ask him what he has to say about these things."

The Christian minister's heart sank. He felt there was no longer a chance of converting the earnest young man and that he had failed. Reared as a Catholic, the student had been taught from an early age to accept the doctrine of Roman Catholicism and to never question it.

A few days later, the young man called and said the priest had been unable to answer his Bible questions. He was leaving the Catholic church. He wanted to become a baptized believer.

> There is no such thing as living in a community where the church cannot grow. The lack of numerical growth in congregations is because of an improper attitude by Christians, not obstacles in the community.

As he baptized his student into the body of Christ, the minister saw a great truth, crystal clear and shining: The conversion of this soul was due to the power of the Word to which he had been exposed, not the minister's efforts in explaining it to him.

From that point forward, the young minister saw evangelism from a whole new—Biblical—perspective. Like Paul, he would sow the Word. The power of God would give the increase.

A lady called to ask me to help her in a Bible study with her future daughter-in-law. When we arrived one bitterly cold New England night, we found the family of her son's fiance dressed to go out in the winter weather.

I assumed they were leaving as a gesture of courtesy to give us a private place to study but later discovered that the real reason for their departure was the desire to not be under the same roof as that "protestant" preacher. They feared that God would put a hex on their home because I had been there for a Bible study. We were successful in baptizing the daughter. However, I wrote off the parents as people who would never be receptive to the Gospel.

Immediately after this, my family and I moved to the Southwest where we worked on a special project before returning to New England two years later. I then had occasion to attend a service at the congregation where my friend and her new daughter-in-law were members.

As I took my seat, I saw a familar face helping with the service. I was thunderstruck. It was the father who had left his home rather than be there when that "protestant" minister came with his "protestant" Bible.

After services I learned that all her family had been converted in the two years I had been gone. Since then, I have never written off anyone as being beyond the power of God's Word.

"I am not ashamed of the gospel, because it is the power of God for the salvation of everyone who believes," Paul wrote in Romans 1:16.

I have learned both from the Bible and from actual experience that we should strive to do the best we can in teaching others and then leave the results up to God. His Word is powerful enough to accomplish whatever needs to be done. We should never worry about whether we can be effective or not. The success of a Bible study will be determined more by the power of the Word of God than by our skill in presenting it.

Someone has said that the Bible is like a lion. A lion does not need to be defended; you just turn him loose, and he will defend himself. The Bible is so powerful that it just needs to be turned loose. It will convert if we will just give it a chance to find fertile, honest hearts.

Let's Get Serious

But first we must get serious about evangelizing our part of the world. We will have to realize that church growth is a problem of attitude, of marketing and of coming to trust the power of God's Word.

A study by a Latin American mission found that the three fastest growing movements there were the Communists, the

Jehovah's Witnesses and the Pentecostal churches. These movements were analyzed for a common denominator. Obviously it was not the message each espoused since one was an anti-Christian ideology, another a cult, and the third viewed as a semi-mainline church.

"The growth of any movement is in direct proportion to its ability to mobilize its entire membership for continuous evangelistic action," was the capsule conclusion of extensive study. Based on this thesis, an evangelistic training program of that fellowship has been moving from country to country in Latin America and experiencing unprecedented church growth.[1]

There is no such thing as a community in which the church cannot grow. The lack of numerical growth in congregations is because of an improper attitude by Christians, not obstacles in the community.

Out of curiosity, I once counted the kernels of corn on an ear of corn. The ear I counted had 374 kernels. The stalk that produced that ear may have even produced another ear with another 374 kernels of corn. But the farmer had planted only one kernel of corn. That one kernel grew and reproduced itself at least 374 times; perhaps 748 times!

If God can do that in the natural world with just one kernel of corn, consider what He can do through us with something as powerful as His Word!

Sneak Preview

Now that you can see that God promises to give you the power to accomplish what He commands, the next learning experience in this study will be to examine an example of evangelizing one-on-one.

Discussion Starters

1. "The power in conversion is in the Word." Do you agree or disagree with this statement? Why?
2. The author says you can grow if you change your thinking patterns. What are your "thinking patterns?"

3. Do you believe they need to change? Why or why not? If so, how do they need to change?
4. How could God evangelize through you specifically?
5. How do you feel about the concept of being able to sell anything (even ridiculous things) in the secular world? Does that translate into our being able to convert people?
6. How do you feel about the way God worked through Moses, David, Gideon, Peter, etc? What does it mean to you, personally?
7. What does the phrase "the power of God" mean in Romans 1:16?
8. What does the illustration of the ear of corn mean to you?

RESPONSE TO THIS CHAPTER

1. For me, the most meaningful part of chapter three is

_____

_____

Why?

_____

2. One thing in chapter three I do not understand is

_____

_____

3. One thing I do not agree with in this chapter is

_____

_____

Why?

_____

4. The one point in this chapter I wish our group could discuss further is

_____

_____

5. Other reactions I have to this chapter are

_____

_____

Notes

1. Leighton Ford. *The Christian Persuader.* (Minneapolis: World Wide Publications, 1966), p. 40.

Part 2

THE BIBLICAL BASIS OF EVANGELISM

The Original Soul-winning Manual

4 THE MODEL SOUL-WINNER

Evangelism - the Life Style of Jesus

CHAPTER HIGHLIGHTS

* Jesus Looked for Opportunities to Talk about Salvation

* Jesus Was Interested in All Who Want to Know the Truth

* Jesus Was Interested in Even the Worst of People

* Jesus Converted, Trained and Sent Out

* Jesus Established Relationships

Jesus is so much the master teacher that attention is riveted on the truth He is presenting, and His method often goes unnoticed. His presentation really conceals the fact that He had a method.

A study of the methods of Jesus is demanded of any student who wishes to know about evangelism and become more evangelistic. Jesus was able to say precisely the right thing in exactly the right way. No one will ever be able to equal His ability, but everyone will find in Him a model to study and follow.

One prime example of the perfect soul-winner at work is Jesus' conversation with the Samaritan woman in John 4. What He told her about salvation was so exciting that she went back to her neighbors full of awe. She had to tell them about this wonderful stranger's message.

A study of the methods of Jesus is demanded of any student who wishes to know about evangelism and become more evangelistic.

Other illustrations of His unique style of personal evangelism can be seen in such stories as Nicodemus, Mary Magdalene, Zacchaeus, Matthew and the lepers.

The primary focus in the Jesus-style of evangelism is on love and salvation. Jesus loved the lost and in each instance did something to encourage understanding and acting upon the Scriptures. Practically everything Jesus said and did had some relevance to evangelism.

In the story of the Samaritan woman, Jesus used a gentle approach that first brushed aside her preconceived notions of racism. Carefully then, He drew this lost soul to Himself, won her confidence, and revealed a way of salvation before He confronted her with the need for a decision.

Re-read the examples of personal work by Christ. Then contemplate the problems Christ had to overcome and the method He used to overcome them.

Jesus Missed No Opportunities

Jesus took advantage of every opportunity to tell people that He had come to offer the world a better life. He looked for opportunities. Jesus stayed attuned to the spiritual needs of people in the world around Him.

When we grasp every chance to discuss the plan of salvation, God will bless the alert with even more opportunities.

This is what Jesus taught in the parable of the talents (Matthew 25:14-30).

Jesus went where the sinners were. He was interested in all individuals. Every time He came in contact with an honest heart, He reached for that person. Spying Zacchaeus in a tree, He took the time to call him down, and to the astonishment of His apostles, invited Himself home for a meal. Jesus explained in more detail in Luke 19:10 after His meal with Zacchaeus, "For the Son of Man came to seek and to save what was lost."

Even at rest, Jesus found an opportunity to teach. We have discussed earlier how He began a conversation with the Samaritan woman over a request for a drink of water.

Outreach is the theme of many of Jesus' parables. Consider the shepherd who would leave 99 sheep that were safe and go looking for the one that was lost.

"Jesus said, 'Father, forgive them, for they do not know what they are doing'" (Luke 23:34) about those who murdered Him. There was no person that Jesus did not try to reach and bring to salvation.

> One man said of himself, "My profession is living for Jesus Christ. I just sell insurance to pay expenses."

Just like Jesus, you and I should always be searching for the one who is lost—not for what that person can do for you, but for what God can do for him. The Christian should always be alert to people around him. He should be sensitive to their needs.

He does this because the Lord has given him the ministry of reconciliation.

> All this is from God, who reconciled us to himself through Christ and gave us the ministry of reconciliation: that God was reconciling the world to himself in Christ, not counting men's sins against them. And he has committed to us the message of reconciliation. We are therefore Christ's ambassadors, as though God were making his appeal through us. We implore you on Christ's behalf: Be reconciled to God (2 Corinthians 5:18-20).

Some scholars believe that the Greek language for "Go ye therefore" (KJV) or "Therefore go" (NIV) in the Great Commission would be translated best "As you are going. . . ." Such a translation would not conflict with other evangelism commands of the New Testament. In actuality, it would reinforce them because Christians are to be making disciples as they go about their normal business.

One man said of himself, "My profession is living for Jesus Christ. I just sell insurance to pay expenses." Paul said, "Make the most of every opportunity" (Colossians 4:5). Jesus was in the people business, and we are in the people business. Personal evangelism is part of our everyday plans, not a specific project we occasionally pursue.

> Making the most of normal contacts calls for some planning . . . But remember to leave the agenda open for the divine appointments the Father will bring your way. Did Jesus gather the disciples around for a morning staff meeting and lay out the day's plans? "All right men, today we will heal two lepers, feed one multitude, deliver one sermon, cast out five demons, and debate three issues with the Pharisees." No, Jesus was apparently content to leave the agenda for the day open. At the same time he was always ready for what came and alert to act in keeping with his purpose. We can trust the Father to use us in surprising ways when we, too, are available and alert.[1]

A husband and his wife attended the services of a congregation in their town one Sunday morning. Afterwards a family invited them home for dinner. On the way home, the husband turned to his host and said, "You know I'm not a Christian, don't you?" Before dinner was over, he had agreed to a Bible study and was baptized in a few weeks. That couple had regularly attended another congregation for more than a year prior to this visit. In that time no one had talked to him to even find out if he was a Christian or not.

Interested in the Religious

Some great religious leaders became disciples in the New Testament: men like Paul, Nicodemus, Cornelius and the Ethiopian Eunuch. These men desired to know the truth. They wanted to do what God asked of them.

Even though the Samaritan woman in John was immoral and disreputable, she was knowledgeable about religious matters, as evidenced by her statements and questions (John

4:12, 20, 25). It was apparent she was caught up in an immoral lifestyle; but for some reason, before Jesus she had no one to teach or encourage her to live a better life.

Opportunities for evangelistic discussions with people who are active in a denomination are generally ignored. Christians mistakenly assume that anyone actively participating in a denomination would not be interested in Bible study. Jesus' assumption, on the contrary, is that these very people are a rich vein to mine spiritually. Usually they are religiously sincere and, more often than not, would welcome an opportunity to learn the truth. This is confirmed in Acts 6:7 when it says that a large number of the Jewish "priests became obedient to the faith."

Jesus Was Interested in the Worst of People

If we had known the Samaritan woman at the time of her conversation with Jesus, we would have identified her as immoral, based on the Biblical description of her. If we were seeking to describe her, we could assume that she was probably attractive. How else could she have gotten five husbands and been able to be live with a sixth man?

We might also assume she was difficult to live with. That's as good an explanation as any for having had five husbands! She may have had a delightful personality when she wanted to have one, and it is probably a safe assumption that she did not have a thimbleful of character.

> The church that does not win, train and send out today is not in the complete soul winning business. . . .

But she was reachable, teachable and changeable because Jesus took the time to see deep inside her, all the way to her honest and sincere heart.

A careful examination of the background of some of Jesus' followers in the New Testament reveal some formerly rough characters. Before meeting Jesus, several might have stolen everything they legally could.

The same is true today. Some of the great saints today were formerly alcoholics, addicts, atheists, prostitutes, liars, thieves, murderers and even satan worshippers—people we might tend to write off as extremely poor prospects.

Jesus had the ability then, and does now through His Word, to change the very worst of people into the very best of Christians. Jesus had "good news" and hope. He addressed the deepest needs of men and showed them a new life and can, through us, do the same today.

The Samaritan woman was probably a down and outer while Nicodemus was an up and outer. Most of the people Jesus healed and preached to were those who endured a hand-to-mouth existence, but many also had substantial means.

Jesus was interested in people in all classes of income. He did not limit His ministry to only one financial or social strata.

Jesus Won, Trained and Sent Out

Jesus was a complete soul-winner. He won people, trained them to teach others, and then sent them out to do it.

The church that does not win, train and send out today is not in the complete soul-winning business and will not be as successful as Jesus was.

The example of Jesus was to send out disciples two by two. He sent out the 70 this way (Luke 10:1). He also sent out the twelve apostles two by two (Mark 6:7).

Most people see in the Great Commission the command to "go" and to "baptize," overlooking the "make disciples of every creature" (Matthew 28:18, 19). The command to "make disciples" means that those who go and win others are to make of these new converts people like themselves who will be constrained not only to follow Jesus but to lead others to follow Him.

After Jesus cast the legion of demons out of the Gezrasene man, the healed man begged to become one of his disciples and go with Him. But Jesus would not let him. Instead He instructed him, "Go home to your family and tell them how much the Lord has done for you, and how he has had mercy on you" (Mark 5:19).

Although Jesus had been rejected by the people of that area previously, He was well received when He returned on a later occasion (Luke 8:37-40). Perhaps the work of the former demon-possessed man had influenced the whole region.

The last message from Jesus to His disciples was a charge to go.

> But you will receive power when the Holy Spirit comes on you; and you will be my witnesses in Jerusalem, and in all Judea and Samaria, and to the ends of the earth (Acts 1:8).

.

Jesus Excluded No One

When Jesus started a conversation with the Samaritan woman, she quickly interjected that "the Jews have no dealings with the Samaritans." The Samaritans were half-breeds and the Jews intensely despised them. Since Jesus was a Jew, she could not understand how He could be interested in her. What she found was that the love of Christ and the grace of God leaps over all racial barriers.

The following three Scriptures forever settle the question of what people are excluded from God's message:

> For God so loved the world that he gave his one and only Son, that whoever believes in him shall not perish but have eternal life (John 3:16).

> He said to them, "Go into all the world and preach the good news to all creation. Whoever believes and is baptized will be saved, but whoever does not believe will be condemned" (Mark 16:15,16).

> Then Peter began to speak: "I now realize how true it is that God does not show favoritism but accepts men from every nation who fear him and do what is right" (Acts 10:34,35).

The only conclusion from these verses is that God loves all people equally. He expects His followers to see to it that all men have the opportunity to be saved—skipping no one.

Work at Becoming A People Person

Jesus successfully reached into the hearts of people because He established relationships. How did He do that? This is a lesson Christians must learn. Mike Cope suggestions three ways to do this.[2]

Spend time with people. In Matthew 9 we read about Jesus eating with Matthew. Later in the gospels, He tells Zacchaeus that He will go to his house for a meal. Jesus didn't go to the homes of those men just to eat. More likely Jesus ate so He could spend time with Matthew and Zacchaeus. That time spent eating with them built a bridge to their hearts.

Rebecca Pippert in *Out of the Saltshaker* comments on this side on Jesus.

> My first impression was that Jesus was utterly delightful. He enjoyed people. He liked to go to parties and to weddings. He was the kind of man people invited for dinner. And He came. He went to where they were.[3]

Apply this lesson to everyday life. You might choose to play racquetball, golf, tennis, go fishing, play bridge or one of a thousand other things. But you need to do something with people so relationships can be built with them. Then they will be more likely to listen to you when you share Jesus with them.

Practice hospitality. Jesus could not invite people to His home because He did not have one, but He understood the comfort and social interaction of a home. A home is a family's safe place, the place they flee to in times of trouble and invite their friends to in times of happiness.

Home is one of the best places to discuss the direction or misdirection of one's life. Many times Jesus is described as eating, sitting or reclining. The relaxed atmosphere of a home gave Him the opportunity to do a better job of teaching.

> Jesus successfully reached into the hearts of people because he established relationships.

THE BIBLICAL BASIS OF EVANGELISM

Be available when people hurt. Jesus was a physician to those who suffered spiritual wounds even more than to those who suffered physical problems. You cannot read His life without seeing how His heart went out to the lonely, the fearful, the hungry, the sick, the prisoner, the mistreated, the suffering and the broken-hearted. When your actions demonstrate love, people will be more inclined to listen to you when you want to talk to them about the plan of salvation. The old saying is true that "People won't care how much you know until they know how much you care."

Sneak Preview

No study of evangelism would be complete without studying how the early church grew. Daily, for three years Jesus trained the twelve apostles in evangelism, and daily they watched Him make disciples. After Christ died and returned to Heaven, He left the harvest in the hands of carefully trained men who were now leading and establishing the church by the inspiration of the Holy Spirit. The next chapter deals with what they did.

Discussion Starters

1. Have you known of an instance in which something happened that opened up a teaching opportunity like Jesus used with the Samaritan woman? Describe it for the class.
2. How do you feel about the statement, "My profession is living for Jesus Christ. I just sell insurance to pay expenses."
3. Can you relate an instance when many people were eventually converted because someone took advantage of an opportunity to share the Bible on an occasion when most would have passed it by?
4. Why did Jesus place such emphasis on the training and sending of disciples to teach others? What relation does 2 Timothy 2:2 have to this?
5. How would you describe Jesus' personality? Why?

6. Discuss with your group some practical ways to do the following four things to establish relationships with people.
   A. Spend time with people.
   B. Do things with people
   C. Practice hospitality.
   D. Be available when people hurt.

RESPONSE TO THIS CHAPTER

1. For me, the most meaningful part of chapter one is

   _____

   _____

   Why?

   _____

2. One thing in chapter one I do not understand is

   _____

   _____

3. One thing I do not agree with in this chapter is

   _____

   _____

   Why?

   _____

4. The one point in this chapter I wish our group could discuss further is

   _____

   _____

5. Other reactions I have to this chapter are

   _____

   _____

Notes

1. Wayne McDill, *Making Friends for Christ* (Nashville: Broadman, 1979), p. 80.
2. Mike Cope, *Living In Two Worlds* (Nashville: Christian Communications, 1987), pg. 102-3.
3. Rebecca Pippert, *Out of the Saltshaker* (Downers Grove, IL: Inter-Varsity Press, 1979), p. 35.

5 EVANGELISM IN THE NEW TESTA- MENT CHURCH

"The Word of the Lord Spread Widely and Grew in Power"

CHAPTER HIGHLIGHTS

* We Visit Lydia and the Church in Philippi
* The Early Christians "Filled Jerusalem" with Their Teaching
* Christians in Jerusalem Taught in the Temple, in Their Homes, and in the Streets
* The Scope of Evangelism Is Identified

The Bible is replete with examples of the phenomenal growth of the early-day church. How exciting it would be to pay a visit to a church of the first century and to be able to study their methods of evangelism. Obviously, they could tell us how to have an aggressive program of converting the lost, because they had one. It would probably be an amazing adventure.

For instance, if we visited the church in Philippi, we

would undoubtedly stay at the home of Lydia, a business woman who helped found the church there. Instead of a servant, somehow I envision that she would greet us at the door with a simple "Welcome, brother." You would find an atmosphere of Christian love tempered with a desire to serve.

"A brother in Christ is my spiritual kinsman, and we share a special love," she might say, taking your children into her arms. "We are family, and my home is yours."

You know how the Philippian church was founded. But you still can not resist asking this special woman how it all started here.

"I was born a Jew but lived in Philippi because of my business. I sought out fellow believers. Fortunately, I found a few Jewish women still faithful to Jehovah God. Sadly, there were no Jewish men to lead us in worship. So we did the best we could, gathering every Sabbath in a quiet place by the river to worship our Creator.

How did they do it? What was their secret?

"God blessed us by hearing our prayers. Can you imagine our joy when one Sabbath a Jewish man joined us to worship God? We learned that our example must have impressed someone because this man was looking for a synagogue and he was directed to us.

"To our amazement, he did not worship according to the Law of Moses. Instead, he started telling us about a man named Jesus. Even in Phillipi we had heard about the "rabble-rouser" claiming to be the king of the Jews. We had assumed that He wasn't or God would have been with Him and not let Him die on that cross.

"But Paul used the Scriptures. He explained that this Jesus Christ was the Messiah of prophecy. You can't begin to understand how astonished I was to discover that this tenderhearted man Paul was the same Saul of Tarsus who had been killing the followers of Jesus Christ.

"Paul explained that he came to us because of our Jewish heritage to tell about his own conversion.

"He continued to use the sacred Scriptures to prove his

points. He told us about seeing Christ on the road to Damascus. He told us about being baptized by Ananias. As the day unfolded, I recognized the truthfulness of his reasoning and the honesty of his heart. Jesus Christ was the Messiah!

"I was baptized, along with my household, that day."

"What happened to Paul after that?"

"Paul stayed in my home while he was preaching and establishing the Lord's church in Philippi. What an exciting time of my life, especially the privilege of having Paul here, right where you're seated. He never let it get dull while he was in town. I've never seen anyone grab every opportunity to teach like Paul did."

"Many opposed him because of what he preached. There was even a riot, but many were converted."

"Could we visit with members of the congregation while we are here? Could we get them to explain how they convert people?"

"Sure. The church meets here each Lord's Day. I think you will especially be inspired by the jailor, and his family, also. He tells a powerful story, and you can't fight back the tears when he talks about how he felt when he washed the back of a badly beaten Paul and Silas. They not only saved his life, but taught him the plan of salvation through Jesus Christ, a gift of eternal life. He says he still trembles at how close he came to committing suicide.

"You can meet nearly all of them tonight when they gather to worship."

"You don't have a church building?"

"I don't suppose we do. What is a church building?"

Later, as the congregation began to gather.

"Tell me, Epaphroditus, what is the church in Philippi doing to evangelize the people of this area?"

"Oh, we've already done that. Every person in Philippi has been taught that Jesus is Lord and what to do to become a Christian."

"What?" You suspect that maybe there is a little exaggeration at work.

"Sure!" Epaphroditus responds and then pauses. Now it is his turn to be surprised. "Is that unusual?"

"How did you accomplish that? You don't have television

or radio or newspapers. Did you have a lot of gospel meetings with Silas, Timothy or Apollos or some of the other outstanding preachers?"

"No. As you know from reading Acts, we tried mass meetings, but most of the time we were put in jail," the former jailor answers.

"Then how did you accomplish such a feat?"

"Don't you know?" another Christian interjects eagerly. "We visited every home in the city. We asked each person who accepted Christ to immediately go to his relatives and friends and tell them the good news we had found. Paul and Silas told us that's the way the church in Jerusalem evangelized that city. The Christians there evangelized the entire city of Jerusalem in a very short time. All the other churches of Asia Minor have followed that example."

"Is that approach effective everywhere?"

"Oh, Yes!" Lydia respond excitedly. "The gospel is having so much impact that some of the pagan religious leaders fear their own religions will die out. When Paul left us, he urged us to remain faithful to this method. Actually, he told us it was the way God wanted it; you know, each one teach as many as possible. After all, it is the least we can do to show our gratitude to Christ."

> The early Christians were so thrilled with the Good News that they continued their teaching even when they were being persecuted because of it.

"Brothers and sisters, this is amazing! Why, at this rate, maybe in the lifetimes of your children or perhaps your grandchildren, the gospel will be able to spread throughout this whole region," you enthuse, impressed, to say the least.

"Haven't you heard," Epaphroditus broke in. "Christians have already taken the gospel to all the people of Asia Minor and Macedonia—both Jews and Gentiles."

"Why, that's impossible. You can't mean everyone!" But you know this is no exaggeration.

"Yes, everyone."

"But that would include Corinth, Ephesus, Athens, Thessalonica, dozens of large cities and hundreds of smaller towns and villages! How long did it take the church to reach all of those people?"

"Not long—just a few years. The same thing is happening in North Africa and Europe. The gospel has reached Spain, too," Lydia interjects. "We have heard of a land called England, and several Christians may have reached there. We hope to have fulfilled the great commission of Jesus before the close of the century."

"I can't believe this. What you are telling me is incredible. You have done more in a generation than we have done in hundreds of years."

"That's strange," Lydia said. "It was really simple for us to do. How can spreading the good news about Jesus have moved so slowly for you? Maybe you're going about it the wrong way."

"Yes," continued Epaphroditus. "Or perhaps the Christians of your generation are not really committed to Jesus."

In 300 years, the gospel was not only preached to the whole world but the whole Roman political empire was undercut and overthrown by the power of the Gospel. The Word on the lips of Christ-conscious disciples crossed seas and deserts and pierced the darkest jungles. The gospel seeped into every city and town and finally into the senate and the very palace of Rome itself until the emperor himself claimed allegiance to Christ.

> "You know that I have not hesitated to preach anything that would be helpful to you but have taught you publicly and from house to house."
> —Paul

In light of historical evidence, does it concern you to compare the slow, plodding spread of the gospel in today's world of lightning-fast communication to the lightning-fast spread of the gospel in a world of plodding communication.

How did they do it? What was their secret? Why is it that

in the book of Acts the outreach of Christians seemed so vibrant and natural, while evangelism today is often forced, dutiful and unnatural?

The answer lies in the first chapter of Acts. Jesus' last communication with His apostles, He offered both reassurance and a commission. He told them they would receive the reassuring power of the Holy Spirit and that they were to "Be my witnesses in Jerusalem, and in all Judea and Samaria, and to the ends of the earth" (Acts 1:8). This identified the means and the scope of their evangelism.

Wayne McDill writes about this passage:

> In the widening circles named in this familiar passage, we first see a pattern of **geography**—from the home city, to the surrounding province, to the next province, to the last place on earth. This may also be interpreted as a **plan** for evangelism and missions, beginning at home and moving outward systematically to the entire world.

> The enlarging pattern of responsibility in this verse could also be interpreted in terms of **relationship.** As we see how these geographical entities were perceived by the Jews of that day, we can see the application to us. You shall be my witnesses, Jesus said, to Jerusalem, your own household. To Judea, your **neighbor.** To Samaria, your **enemy.** To the remotest part of the earth, your **stranger.** From the strongest relationship to the weakest, the witness is to be borne on a person-to-person basis.[1]

Evidently their efforts were successful because in Acts 5:28 the high priest said to them, "You have filled Jerusalem with your teaching." How they were able to fill Jerusalem with their teaching is identified in Acts 5:42.

> Day after day, in the temple courts and from house to house, they never stopped teaching and proclaiming the good news that Jesus is the Christ.

What kind of response did their teaching have? That is described in the next chapter.

> So the word of God spread. The number of disciples in Jerusalem increased rapidly, and a large number of priests became obedient to the faith (Acts 6:7).

New Testament evangelism had a built-in accelerator. The

early Christians were so thrilled with the Good News that they continued their teaching even when they were being persecuted because of it. Acts 8:4 says that, "Those who had been scattered preached the word wherever they went." It is probable that great congregations, even Antioch of Syria, were planted by these unknown, ordinary Christians from ordinary walks of life who were forced from their previous homes by persecution in Jerusalem.

A diagram of the evangelism activities of the early church in Acts would be:

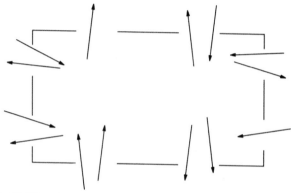

J. B. Phillips imaginatively pictures a couple of angels in Heaven watching earth. The angels observe a flash of brilliant light. This light glows very brightly for a short while and then goes out. Then it flashes again and separates into thousands of smaller lights that cover the entire planet.

One of the angels explains to the other that the first light was the earthly life of Jesus. Then He was killed, and the light went out. But He arose from the dead and dispersed His light to many others at Pentecost, and it eventually spread in thousands of directions across the dark planet.[2]

Read the New Testament description of how the church grew through the preaching of Paul and the other disciples.

Paul entered the synagogue and spoke boldly there for three months, arguing persuasively about the kingdom of God. But some of them became obstinate; they refused to believe and publicly maligned the Way. So Paul left them. He took the disciples with him and had discussions daily in the lecture hall of Tyrannus. This went on for two years, so that all the Jews and Greeks who lived in the province of Asia heard the word of the Lord.

In this way the word of the Lord spread widely and grew in power (Acts 19:8-10, 20).

Another passage that tells us a lot about the early disciples' enthusiasm and methods is Acts 20:20: "You know that I have not hesitated to preach anything that would be helpful to you but have taught you publicly and from house to house."

Some Conclusions

Some definite conclusions about the Christians of the first century and the growth of the early church can be drawn from reading these passages.
- They were in love with God.
- They were involved with people.
- They possessed a faith that knew no bounds.
- They felt the urgent necessity of each one winning one—and they didn't stop there.
- They were more concerned about souls than about earthly possessions.
- They believed the world was lost.
- They were so filled with the message of salvation they had to tell it.
- Their dedicated lives attracted the world.

The fact that the Bible deals extensively with the content of the gospel, but is relatively silent about the techniques and structures of evangelism is significant. The Scripture seems to leave us free to choose our own methods. We have only a handful of clues about what specific methods those first century Christians used. The one thing we are told clearly is that the gospel soon spread to all the world because the early Christians shared it freely everywhere they went.

Sneak Preview

While we may support all that has been studied, we must still grapple with the "Moses Phenomenon." "I just don't have the ability to set up and conduct evangelistic Bible studies." How many times has that been said? But the Lord has a mission for each Christian just as He did for Moses. Are we willing to let God change and use us?

Discussion Starters

1. What differences do you see between the evangelism of the church in Acts and our churches today? List them. What similarities are there?
2. What do you think the churches in Acts had that enabled them to evangelize so effectively?
3. The persecution of the church only seemed to encourage their evangelistic efforts. Why? Do we face persecution today? Does it affect our evangelism?
4. What can we learn from the failure and success of Paul's work in Acts 19:8-20?

REPONSE TO THIS CHAPTER

1. For me, the most meaningful part of chapter five is

_____

_____

Why?

_____

2. One thing in chapter five I do not understand is

_____

_____

3. One thing I do not agree with in this chapter is

_____

_____

Why?

_____

4. The one point in this chapter I wish our group could discuss further is

_____

_____

5. Other reactions I have to this chapter are

_____

_____

Notes

1. Wayne McDill, *Making Friends for Christ* (Nashville: Broadman Press, 1979), p. 27.
2. J. B. Phillips, *New Testament Christianity* (London: Hodder & Stoughton, 1956), p. 21.

Part 3

THE WILLINGNESS TO BE CHANGED

Are You Stuck in a Rut?

6 THE POTENTIAL YOU HAVE TO BECOME

The Lord Isn't Through With Me Yet

CHAPTER HIGHLIGHTS

* When Jesus Changed Simon's Name to Peter, He Was Making More Than A Name Change

* We Can Change—Nothing Locks Us in Old Failures

* We Should See the Potential in Others and in Ourselves

* Change is Necessary, Painful and Inevitable

* The Lord Wants To Change Us

President Jackson:

The canal system of this country is being threatened by the spread of a new form of transportation known as railroads. The federal government must preserve the canals for the following reasons.

One, if boats are supplanted by railroads, serious unemployment will result. Captains, cooks, drivers, hostlers, repairmen and lock tenders will be left without means of livelihood, not to mention the numerous farmers now employed in growing hay for horses.

Two, boat builders would suffer and towline, whip, and harness makers would be left destitute.

Three, canal boats are absolutely essential to the defense of the United States. In the event of the expected trouble with England, the Erie Canal would be the only means by which we could ever move the supplies so vital to waging modern war.

As you may well know, Mr. President, railroad carriages are pulled at the enormous speed of 15 miles per hour by engines which, in addition to endangering life and limb of passengers, roar and snort their way through the countryside, setting fire to crops, scaring the livestock and frightening women and children. The Almighty certainly never intended that people should travel at such a breakneck speed.

> Sincerely Yours,
> Martin Van Buren
> Governor of New York

> Disciples of Jesus need to be aware that a desire to develop the image of Christ may often bring about change that will be necessary and painful.

This letter dramatically illustrates the fear of change, a negative attitude that often hinders the progress of social development. In light of the mechanized advances of today's modern world, the fears seem ridiculous, but they were all very real to Martin Van Buren, who even called on the name of Almighty God to justify his state of alarm.

This world is ever changing. People are alive today who went to town in a buckboard, cooked on a wood stove, and read their Bible by the light of a kerosene lantern. They were born before the development of radio, television, x-ray machines, airplanes, heart bypass surgery, penicillin or even something as common as the ball point pen. And be assured, happenstance of birth will not keep them from enjoying the benefit of a changing world. Change is a part of life. One second after birth, change begins and continues occurring until the last big change, death.

If change is such a natural, normal occurrence, then why is it so difficult for us to change?

God's Still Working On Me

I liked this message on a T-shirt that was popular a few years ago; "The Lord isn't through with me yet." That is a good slogan because of what it said about the person wearing it. That person in the T-shirt realized that there was a supreme power helping him to change for the better. That T-shirt owner knew that all things are possible with the Lord, even the ability to change to become the soul-winning person the Lord wants us to be.

A great story about change that has some good lessons for us is found in John 1:35-42.

> The next day John was there again with two of his disciples. When he saw Jesus passing by, he said, "Look, the Lamb of God!" When the two disciples heard him say this, they followed Jesus. Turning around, Jesus saw them following and asked, "What do you want?" They said, "Rabbi" (which means Teacher), "where are you staying?" "Come," he replied, "and you will see." So they went and saw where he was staying, and spent that day with him. It was about the tenth hour. Andrew, Simon Peter's brother, was one of the two who heard what John had said and who had followed Jesus. The first thing Andrew did was to find his brother Simon and tell him, "We have found the Messiah" (that is, the Christ). Then he brought Simon to Jesus, who looked at him and said, "You are Simon son of John. You will be called Cephas" (which, when translated, is Peter).

This is the only time Jesus changed the name of one of His disciples. This was not because He did not like the name Simon but to make a point.

Having just met Jesus and only equipped with the accepted teaching of the times on the coming Messiah, Simon probably didn't understand what affect the Lord was about to have on his life. What affect do you think it had on Simon for the Lord to change his name upon their first meeting?

Some people change names because they hate the one

they have, like the Indian who was named "Chief Screeching Train Whistle." He changed it to "Toots."

Other people like their names. In our time, some women keep their maiden name even after marriage. For instance, if Jane Black married John Smith and kept her maiden name, she would become Jane Black-Smith!

Names used to have meaning. A person who worked with gold could be named Goldsmith. When Jesus changed Simon's name to Peter, the Lord was telling this fisherman that changes would become necessary.

Peter's temperament is a good example. The Bible illustrates it as sometimes being unstable and reckless. He seemed prone to impetuous violence. When the Lord was arrested, Peter was not averse to using his sword—with enthusiasm, if not accuracy.

Peter's new name signaled a character change. But it would take months—even the crucible of Christ's death—before the dynamic spiritual leader would appear.

Simon's new name became Cephas, which is Aramaic. The Greek equivalent of Cephas is Petros. We know him as Peter, which is the English translation of Petros, both Petros and Peter meaning rock.

Peter would later realize that this name change indicated not only the direction of the change in his life but the extent of that change. Until Christ began to work on him, Peter's life could be described more as shifting sand than rock, a condition that existed even until after Calvary. The change in Simon's life to something resembling a rock would be a transformation of major proportions.

Grabbing the Bar

When comparing our life with God's Word, we should want to change and become what God wants us to be. No power, not even that of Satan, can force us to remain timid about sharing the gospel. By the grace and power of God, we can change. No one forces us to remain mired in the muck of old failures.

By becoming Christians, we have already dared to accept

the challenge of building a new life. However, the committment must carry over into evangelism.

This takes full committment, like that shown by the trapeze artist in the circus. The trapeze bar is his security. When another trapeze bar swings into his view, he is faced with a dilemma. Should he relinquish the bar he holds and turn loose of his security? Should he reach for the new bar? There comes a moment of truth, because he realizes that if he grabs onto the new bar, he must release the old one. When new committment is made, it must be a total committment.

During the three years of Jesus ministry, Peter showed little evidence of change. But due to the immense patience of Jesus progress did occur.

> A Christian should be constantly growing. He should be a different person now than he was three years ago.

The slowness with which major change occurs in Peter is illustrative of the seemingly cold-molasses speed of great character accomplishments. A mother once said that parents often refer to their children as clay to be molded but that her children were more like granite blocks to be chiseled. Many of us Christians may be like that child! But once God chisels that granite, He really has something.

After the crucifixion and resurrection, Peter did become that rock Christ predicted. To the believers in the Roman provinces for whom life had become difficult and was probably going to get worse, Peter encouraged them:

> And the God of all grace, who called you to his eternal glory in Christ, after you have suffered a little while, will himself restore you and make you strong, firm and steadfast (1 Peter 5:10).

The words "strong, firm and steadfast" do not describe the stuff that Simon was originally made of, but it now described the rock whom Jesus had fashioned from such unpromising material.

The Power to Become

When Jesus looked at someone like Simon, He saw the potential of this person to become something greater. We should attempt to see like Jesus. When a Christian looks at others, and especially himself, he should not be content with what he sees on the surface. He should probe deeper to see the potential buried under human frailties. What we are now is not nearly as important as what we have the power to become.

> Disciples of Jesus need to be willing to have their attitudes changed. They need to be willing to rearrange their thinking in order to follow Jesus and to become what He wants them to be.

An architect had taken a piece of raw, undeveloped land and built a showpiece of a golf course. He joined a group of preachers trying out the course, and one of them asked how the beautiful course was created. The architect explained that he had taken a picture of the land from an airplane before he checked, in great detail, every specific of the topography—the soil, the water supply and the drainage. He had made detailed measurements, innumerable plans and drawn up various scenarios for this course before selecting the perfect one. Finally, the earth movers began. Before long it looked like World War III had been fought on that land, but soon a beautiful golf course emerged. The architect added that work on the course would never be finished because constant care would be lavished on it to keep out the weeds and vines. Without constant vigilance, the course would disappear.

Don't Make Me Bleed

This need for change caused crisis moments in Peter's life. It was not an easy task to change Simon into Peter. The willingness to change must exist, and this is where real discipleship begins.

When a recent president campaigned for office, he promised to get big government off the back of citizens and to trim the fat from the federal budget. When he was elected, many of the people who had backed his candidacy soon realized these changes could not be made without cost. Some had seen only the goal and not the process, so they were surprised when changes affected them, sometimes adversely.

In a political cartoon, the president was pictured as a surgeon with a scapel in his hand bending over John Doe on the operating table. The patient is saying, "Cut and slash, Doctor, but don't make me bleed."

Disciples of Jesus need to be aware that a desire to develop the image of Christ may often bring about **change that will be necessary and painful.** Like the trapeze artist, it will require total committment. And like the Lord's patient shaping of Peter, it may occur one tiny step at a time.

The Inevitability of Change

The definition of a disciple is "a follower." Discipleship may take a person where he has never been. At the very least, he will be led to a point of spiritual development that did not exist when the committment began.

A Christian should be constantly growing. He should be a different person now than he was three years ago. How discouraging to discover that twenty years had produced no improvement.

A Christian should be able to chart spiritual growth from year to year. Perhaps some decision has been made based on a deeper understanding of the Scripture. Perhaps a soul has been led to Christ. No better way exists to grow spiritually than to teach others the Good News of salvation. And there is no better way for a Christian to chart his own spiritual growth than to worship beside a new babe that he helped introduce to the Lord.

Not In My Concrete

A man poured a concrete sidewalk in front of his house. He came back in an hour or so to look at it and noticed the footprints of some children in his newly poured concrete. Finding the neighborhood children, he told them exactly what he thought about that. One of the neighbors listening to all of this said to him later, "Why did you talk to those children like that? I thought you loved kids." He replied, "I love them in the abstract, but not in my concrete."

We may love more in the abstract than in the concrete. Change may be one of those. Before Jesus told Simon that He would make him a fisher of men, Peter probably thought of himself as a self-made man and proud of his creation. But after three years with Jesus, he was no longer the opinionated and strong-willed person Jesus first met.

The main reason we resist good changes is stubborn pride. And to resist change that God seeks is especially horrendous, particularly in Christians.

Sometimes elders will counsel people, pointing out that specific problems will not improve until a lifestyle change occurs that will eliminate the source of the problem. In most cases, people resist these suggestions to change. Because of stubborn pride, they are not willing to allow anyone to take over their lives and affect changes—sadly, not even the Lord!

> If you are going to grow, you have to be willing to move into new and challenging areas.

Counselors see many couples whose marriages are floundering because of obvious sin, but are resistant to change. There is no way they are going to be dependent upon someone else, even God, for the salvation of their marriage. These stiff-necked people would rather be divorced than to change their comfortable ways.

Disciples of Jesus need to be open to having their attitudes changed. They need to be willing to rearrange their thinking in order to follow Jesus and to become what He wants them to be.

The Cost of Discipleship

Jesus indicated to His first followers that they would experience marked changes in the direction of their lives when they began a disciple-teacher relationship with Him. He was going to make all of them "fishers of men."

Some of those disciples knew about being a fisher of fish. They knew that they did not always do so well. All fishermen have days when the fish do not cooperate. So to move from fishing for fish to fishing for men may have sounded exciting. But it could have also sounded somewhat intimidating.

They had never fished for men before. What if they were not good at it? Fish do not answer back when you try to catch them; Galileans would. They realized that it would involve sacrifice—hours of travel and long periods of time away from home. Parallel changes occur in the lives of all who follow Jesus as they strive to be the best possible disciples. If you are going to grow, you have to be willing to move into new and challenging areas. Challenges often produce apprehension since they are usually an adventure into the unknown. But we must remember that the Christian adventure is orchestrated by the Lord. You will be in His hands and in His program.

Are You Willing?

"I can't teach others." That is the most commonly heard excuse for not being evangelistic and that is exactly the point of this lesson.

Few Christians teach because they have a natural knack and it comes easy. But all Christians can teach if they are willing to change and utilize what natural talents they have. A Christian can learn how to teach because, like Peter, he can be changed by the Lord. The Lord can move an inactive Christian into the sweat and strain of the harvest field if the Christian is ready to allow the change to occur.

The Lord sees us, like Peter, for what we can become. Peter could not conceive the great works he could and would do when he began to follow Christ. It was years before he truly understood what it was to become a fisherman of men.

Unlike Peter, the challenge is clear to today's Christian, who does not have to wait for God's plan to be revealed. Christians must be changed into soul-winners because the harvest field is white and waiting. God is counting on us! There are great works to be done. Souls to be saved. A judgment to come.

Sneak Preview

If you are at the point where you are willing to change your present lifestyle and be used as a soul-winner for Jesus, then the next step is to find someone to teach. Where are the souls to be harvested? The people at work and in your neighborhood do not seem to be interested in religion. The next chapter describes how to present the gospel to people who are not interested in it.

Discussion Starters

1. Explain what lessons we can learn from the statement, "The first thing Andrew did was to find his brother Simon and tell him, 'We have found the Messiah' . . . Then he brought Simon to Jesus."
2. Why was Peter's life changed so dramatically after the crucifixion and resurrection? How can this relate to us?
3. What can we learn from the fact it took so long for a character change to occur in Peter? Do we change fast or slowly?
4. What is an example of a change that was difficult in your own life?
5. Do you feel comfortable making major changes in your life? When do you feel most comfortable? Least comfortable? Why?
6. What changes would the Lord have to make in you for you to feel secure in being a "fisher of men"?
7. What would be the cost of change in your life?

RESPONSE TO THIS CHAPTER

1. For me, the most meaningful part of chapter six is

_____

_____

Why?

_____

2. One thing in chapter six I do not understand is

_____

_____

Why?

_____

3. One thing I do not agree with in this chapter is

_____

_____

Why?

_____

4. The one point in this chapter I wish our group could discuss further is

_____

_____

5. Other reactions I have to this chapter are

_____

_____

Part 4

MARKETING
THE CHURCH

How to Promote the Gospel

7 THE PACKAGING OF THE PRODUCT

The Gospel Has Not Changed but the World Has

CHAPTER HIGHLIGHTS

* We Need to Be Relevant in Packaging Our Presentation of the Gospel
* Methods Must Change as Times Change
* The Connection Between Relationships and Church Affiliation
* People Are Brought to Jesus by People

Joe was introduced to Janet after a volleyball game at the Young Professionals class picnic one hot, muggy Saturday afternoon. She was dissheveled, her hair windblown, and she wore no makeup. A baggy sweatshirt and blue jeans with a hole in the knee completed her mismatched ensemble. With a quick welcome Joe darted off to join his group of friends.

The next morning in Bible class, he could not keep from covertly examining a young woman visiting the class. He was even more pleased when the teacher identified her as a new class member. She had just moved to town.

When the teacher identfed her as Janet, Joe could not believe his eyes. She did not appear to be the same person he had met the day before. Today, she looked like a million dollars. The hairdo was fantastic, makeup was carefully applied, and the dress she was wearing was stunning. This time Joe made sure he stayed around to talk awhile when he was introduced the second time. When attraction collides with human nature, something happens.

This same principle works for Christianity.

> Teach slaves to be subject to their masters in everything, to try to please them, not to talk back to them, and not to steal from them, but to show that they can be fully trusted, so that in every way they will make the teaching about God our Savior attractive (Titus 2:9, 10).

Christians have to be relevant in their presentation of the gospel. . . .

Packaging leads to appreciation, whether it is interest in an attractive girl or an attractive Christian life. Slaves were told to set an example in their personal lives so that their masters would appreciate their Godly lives and be attracted to Christianity.

Repackaging is Sometimes Necessary

Christians have to be relevant in their presentation of the gospel or efforts at evangelism will more often fail than succeed.

No matter how sumptuous the food, if the tables in a restaurant are almost as dirty as the floor, if flies dive-bomb the food, or if the employees act disinterested in patrons, that place will soon go out of business. But it would not take much effort for a sharp manager to clean the place up, eliminate the bugs, and train the workers to be courteous, friendly and efficient. The food has not changed, but its presentation has.

God's theology cannot be changed by man. Christians have no right to change it. Only God can do that, and He has elected not to do so. So, as secular advertising people would say, "We must change the packaging."

Evangelism presents a problem for some because of past mistakes. "Evangelism" suggests critical, high-pressure and a mentality which, since the turn of the century, has made people uncomfortable.

Some of the methods borrowed from the secular principles of salesmanship have even caused dissillusionment with the message. People occasionally perceive of evangelism as a manipulation of human fears through the principles of salesmanship. Unfortunately, these high pressure techniques have created a leery attitude toward the Good News and the ideal of "evangelizing" one's neighbor. The message is still worthwhile; the packaging has just been poor.

As James Thompson has asked, "How does the church present the good news to a culture that seems to be innoculated against it?"[1] To be successful in converting people, Christians have to figure out how to present the Bible so the world will accept it rather than reject it.

It is similar to the old dilemma of the man who wanted to impress his lady friend. He decided to tell her she was so beautiful, that when he was with her, "time stood still." But what he said was that she had "a face that would stop a clock."

We achieve those same results sometimes by the approach we use in contacting people about being lost and needing to be saved. Our goal must be to describe the gospel of Jesus in ways that are clearly relevant to contemporary circumstances and tensions without minimizing the hard truths that He taught and demanded of us.

Change the Method—Not the Message

In our struggle to offer real, practical biblical solutions, we should realize that some of the traditional strategies for sharing our faith will no longer work. The message is the same, but the world has changed. We have to be wise enough to analyze our environment and provide creative responses to its challenges.

Typically, congregations are at least five to ten years behind society in responding to population transitions. Unless

Christians develop insightful strategies for redirecting evangelism efforts, congregations of the future may become totally ineffective, if well-intentioned, institutions indistinguishable from other religious groups. We must be sensitive to both our culture and the Bible, adapting our approaches without compromising our message. I think this is what Paul meant when he wrote:

> Though I am free and belong to no man, I make myself a slave to everyone, to win as many as possible. To the Jews I became like a Jew, to win the Jews. To those under the law I became like one under the law (though I myself am not under the law), so as to win those under the law. To those not having the law I became like one not having the law (though I am not free from God's law but am under Christ's law), so as to win those not having the law. To the weak I became weak, to win the weak. I have become all things to all men so that by all possible means I might save some. I do all this for the sake of the gospel, that I may share in its blessings (1 Corinthians 9:19-23).

> "How does the church present the good news to a culture that seems to be innoculated against it?"
> —James Thompson

We must dedicate ourselves to proclaiming the gospel in new ways that are relevant to people's lives. For example, many people now live in apartment and condominium complexes with guards at the gate. No one gets in; no salesman, and no Christian trying to knock on doors to establish Bible classes.

A large percentage of women work and therefore no one is at home during the day. Those who are home are extremely hesitant to answer to the knock of a stranger. Single women almost never open their doors to someone they don't know.

Technology is increasingly providing protection and privacy for people. A machine is now available that will block incoming calls from telephone numbers that have not been preprogrammed as acceptable by the homeowner. So how do you reach these people?

Exciting New Church Growth Research

A vast amount of academic research has been done in the field of church growth in recent years. The thrust of this research has been on what will work, what has worked, and what does not work. If we want to win as many souls as possible, we should take advantage of this hard-earned information.

Cold Canvassing

Years ago, cold canvassing for Bible studies would work well in certain parts of the country. Rural people busy in the back part of the house would commonly call out, "Come on in—the door's open" in response to a knock. They had no idea who was at the door, but the visitor was welcome anyway.

However, in recent years college students selling Bibles from door-to-door during summer break have been introduced to a whole new world. More often than not on the first call of the year, the door is slammed in a salesman's face by an angry homeowner who did not want to be disturbed. And things go down hill from there.

A successful personal evangelism director was once explaining that door-knocking does not work anymore. He had been with campaign workers who knocked on doors, present one lesson, and baptize a hundred people. But when the workers went back the next year, they could find only about five of those who had been baptized. The rest had drifted back into the world. Obviously, the new converts from this method of evangelism were not lasting.

Rejection is No Fun!

Besides, many Christians just cannot force themselves to go door-knocking in an effort to find people interested in studying the Bible. They fear that most homeowners view their attempts to spread the gospel as a bothersome intrusion by religious fanatics. The average resident sees very little distinction between the Mormons, the Jehovah's Witnesses, the Seventh Day Adventists and Christians.

Others will not go door-knocking because they have tried and never been successful at it. They feel defeated even before they start. Inevitably they will encounter some antagonistic people who consider them an intrusion. The rejection rate quickly discourages the Christian, and this leads to a rapid dropout in the evangelism program based on door-knocking. Very few people can hear the word "no" ten times out of every eleven times they knock on the door and still press forward eagerly.

> ## The message is the same, but the world has changed.

What is missing in door-knocking is a prior personal connection from which a Christian has an understanding of a prospect's personal needs. In order to engage in a meaningful religious dialogue with a non-Christian, prior personal connection is invaluable. Even the persistent door-to-door salesmen who used to peddle everything from encyclopedias to liniment are extremely rare in today's computerized society because the method is outdated.

A few Christians can cold canvass successfully perhaps; and if they prefer to work this way, they should be encouraged. But for most people, another method needs to be found

Two Keys to Growth

Congregational growth experts believe there are two principles which spur growth. First, a congregation should find the hurts in the community and heal them. Second, a congregation that is growing and increasing its membership is doing so by conversions gained through neighborhood Bible studies.

Church growth research has also proven that relationships are the major reason people will eventually affiliate with a church. The vast majority of new converts identify a "relational factor" as being responsible for their church membership. This means that a friend, relative or neighbor influenced them to come as opposed to a stranger. Friendship ties were mentioned more often than kinship ties. Only a small percentage responded to a "content oriented" presentation of the gospel.

The New Testament records 40 instances of suffering people having been healed by Jesus. Thirty-four of those people were either brought to Jesus by a friend or Jesus was taken to them. In only six of the 40 cases did the sufferers find their way to Christ without assistance.

Relationships Are Vital

Is the percentage any different today? Of the vast number of people who come to Jesus, most of them will reach Him because of the interest and cooperation of a friend, one who is genuinely interested and concerned about their spiritual welfare.

The Christian faith today usually spreads through an interpersonal influence, especially that of new Christians. That is how most new ideas or products spread in a society. We may initially learn of a new possibility from a media message, but we usually adopt it only after it has been made credible and recommended by a trusted person.

The Institute of American Church Growth polled 4,000 people as to how they were influenced to first attend the services of the church where they eventually become converts.[2] These statistics were found:

- 2% - 3% just walked in
- 2% - 3% came through the church's programs
- 5% - 6% were attracted by the preacher
- 1% - 2% came out of a special need
- 1% - 2% were reached through visitation by church members
- 4% - 5% came through a Sunday School class
- ½ of 1% came through a public evangelistic crusade
- 75% to 90% were converted through the influence of friends and relatives

Who are these relatives and friends? They are:

- Family members—a spouse, parents, grandparents, aunts, uncles, cousins, in-laws, nephews, nieces
- Neighbors
- Elderly friends
- New families in the neighborhood
- Friends through sports and hobbies
- Friends at work
- Especially receptive are any of these people you know who are undergoing personal life stresses of some kind.

How to Win Friends and Influence People

Perhaps a person is not happy with his present relationships and wants to make new friends so that eventually he can help them discover Jesus. Making friends is an art and some are far more gifted at this than others. Author K. C. Hinckley lists four stages of building friendships.[3]

1. **Taking the initiative.**
   - Being the first to say hello.
   - Being friendly.
   - Making small talk.
   - Remembering the other person's name and using it often.
   - Being genuinely interested in him or her.
2. **Establishing rapport.** Rapport is an attitude of mutual acceptance.
   - Thinking in your heart, "I accept you as you are." Like Jesus, I can accept you as having great personal value to God.
   - Listening with interest to what the other person says.
   - Expressing approval; giving compliments where they are due.
   - Being sensitive to specific needs and opportunities where you could serve.
   - Looking for an occasion to invite the other person to join you in some activity.
3. **Being a friend.** Friendship has a price tag: time. It means putting other people first.
   - Listening; being attentive to thoughts and feelings.

- Affirming the other person; expressing what you like about him or her.
- Being transparent; openly expressing your own feelings.
- Letting your friend serve you and do you favors.
- Accepting your friend as he or she is, without trying to reform him or her immediately, before they are ready to consider the possibility of a change.

4. **Building a relationship.**
   - Letting the other person know what you're thinking; allowing that person to see inside you.
   - Seeking the other person's counsel.
   - Sharing your personal resources: money, abilities, and so on.
   - Making time for him or her.
   - Not overdoing it; not trying to control the other person or be possessive.

Friendship is babysitting for emergencies, helping move a heavy appliance, preparing meals in times of illness, shoveling snow or mowing and watering a lawn while a neighbor is on vacation. This is a very sensitive and practical love that would capture the friendship of anyone, and, after all, is just basic Christianity to a born-again believer.

> relationships are the major reason people will eventually affiliate with a church.

Wayne McDill compares these kinds of relationships to a forest of trees and webs of influence.

These webs of influence tie one believer to a host of others who have gone before him and another multitude who come after him. The key is relationship. Though a wide variety of efforts have been made to win people to Christ, the overwhelming majority of converts comes through the influence of family and friends. A Christian's influence is most strongly felt, then, as he reaches out to those in his own world in the natural opportunities he has every day.

Each of us lives in a world unique to himself. No one else, not even your closest relative, knows the same combination of people. This special set of acquaintances is your world, your own everyday mission field. No one can influence this group of people as you can. In a very real sense, you are the key person in their coming to Christ. As you accept responsibility for your world, the Father will do remarkable things in the midst of it.

Tom Wolf has pointed out that the New Testament pattern of evangelism was based on this circle of personal acquaintances. He calls it "oikos evangelism." Oikos is the Greek word for house or household. It was used in the first century to mean the fundamental and natural unit of society, and consisted of one's sphere of influence—his family, friends, and associates. When Peter went to declare the gospel to Cornelius, his whole oikos was there for the message. "Cornelius was waiting for them, and had called together his relatives and close friends, . . . many people" (Acts 10:24, 27).[4]

Again, McDill says:

Though you may be prone to take them for granted, these people you already know are your best possibilities for influencing for Christ. They already know you. They are not suspicious of you as they would be if you were a stranger who approached them. They have the opportunity to observe your life, to see you over the course of weeks and months. They can get in touch with you easily through normal contacts. You are an accepted part of their world. They do not think it odd to have a conversation with you. As a result you are not seen as a threat to their privacy.[5]

The most-believable and best-remembered form of secular advertising is personal testimony. We try a new restaurant because a friend has tried it and recommends it to us.

Bible Examples of Relationships

This is a principle mentioned several times in the New Testament. For instance, Peter was brought to Jesus by his brother, Andrew.

Andrew, Simon Peter's brother, was one of the two who heard what John had said and who had followed Jesus. The first thing Andrew did was to find his brother Simon and tell him, "We have found the Messiah" (that is, the Christ). Then he brought Simon to Jesus (John 1:40-42).

Another illustration of this is when Jesus told the formerly demon-possessed man to

> "Go home to your family and tell them how much the Lord has done for you, and how he has had mercy on you." So the man went away and began to tell in the Decapolis how much Jesus had done for him. And all the people were amazed (Mark 5:19,20).

> This is also how Jesus made such an impact upon the Samaritans. Then, leaving her water jar, the woman went back to the town and said to the people, "Come, see a man who told me everything I ever did. Could this be the Christ?" They came out of the town and made their way toward him.

> Many of the Samaritans from that town believed in him because of the woman's testimony, "He told me everything I ever did." So when the Samaritans came to him, they urged him to stay with them, and he stayed two days. And because of his words many more became believers (John 4:28-30,39,40).

Sneak Preview

The next most relevant question at this point is: How do you reach people that you do not know and will not have an opportunity to develop a friendly relationship with before a Bible study? This will be studied in the closing chapters.

Discussion Starters

1. Have you ever bought a product because of the way it was packaged? Have you ever rejected a product because of its package? Describe the products?
2. Recall the last time you tried something new because a trusted friend recommended it, whether it was a restaurant, a book, etc.
3. What lessons can we learn from the statistics on why people become converts?
4. Why did you come to this church?
5. If it is true that "relationships are the major reason people affiliate with a church," what does that say to us about visitors and new members?

6. What is involved in creating relationships?
7. Name at least one relationship you have that could possibly lead to a Bible study.
8. What are the hurts and needs among your neighbors in your community?
9. Describe your network of relationships, if you have one. How did it form? If you don't have one, how could you develop one?
10. Would you be willing to join an evangelistic teaching program if you were excited about the material you were using?
11. Would you be willing to be involved in an evangelistic teaching program if you had a good method for finding prospective studies?

Areas of My Life in Which I'm Already Involved With Non-Christians
Examples: Work; Boy Scouts; PTA.

Other Areas of My Life in Which I Could Include Non-Christians
Examples: Lunches; Sports Activities; Hobbies.

RESPONSES TO THIS CHAPTER

1. For me, the most meaningful part of chapter seven is

_____

_____

Why?

_____

2. One thing in chapter seven I do not understand is

_____

_____

3. One thing I do not agree with in this chapter is

_____

_____

Why?

_____

4. The one point in this chapter I wish our group could discuss further is

_____

_____

5. Other reactions I have to this chapter are

_____

_____

Notes

1. James Thompson, *The Church in Exile* (Abilene, TX: ACU Press, 1990), p. 46
2. Win and Charles Arn, *The Master's Plan For Making Disciples* (Pasadena, CA: Church Growth Press, 1982), p. 43.
3. K. C. Hinckley, *Living Proof* (Colorado Springs, CO: Navpress, 1990), p. 38, 39.
4. Wayne McDill, *Making Friends For Christ* (Nashville: Broadman Press, 1979), p. 29.
5. Ibid., p. 79.

8 | HOW TO REACH RECEPTIVE PEOPLE

Positioning Ourselves for Evangelism

CHAPTER HIGHLIGHTS

* How to Find Someone to Teach
* Prayer Indispensable in Disciple-Making
* Multitudes Are Waiting for Someone to Ask them to Be Part of a church
* The Ripest of All Groups for Evangelism Is Young People
* We Need to Be Innovative in Our Evangelistic Thinking
* What We Must Learn in Order to Convert the Lost

Jim Slouched in the chair in front of the minister's desk, obviously discouraged.

"George," he said. "I have thoroughly studied the plan of salvation in the Bible to prepare myself to teach the lost. I have bought and read all of the books I can find on personal evangelism. I feel I am prepared mentally and spiritually to teach the lost."

He continued, "I feel it is my responsibility as a Christian to be evangelistic. My problem is that I don't have any prospects with whom I could hold a Bible study. I haven't ever converted anyone, because I don't know how to find someone to teach."

Unfortunately the world has few men with as open and honest hearts as the Ethiopian Eunuch or Cornelius or the Samaritan woman. In an ideal world, people would flock to the church building demanding Bible studies or be lined up at the door an hour before Sunday worship.

But this is not an ideal world. Even Christians have trouble getting to the church building on time. In a materialistic world, the emphasis is on possessions and self-indulgence, not sacrifice and self-denial. So Christians must search out those to teach. They must be alert to every opportunity because the world will not come to them.

Very few Christians have ever encountered someone looking for the truth. I can only remember one person coming to me, and I am convinced that a lot of conversation with someone preceded that request. So how does a Christian find someone to teach?

The Importance of Prayer

First, and foremost, pray! Prayer is a vital part of the soul-winning process. It is the key that will unlock opportunities.

Remember the examples of Jesus and Paul? Jesus wept over lost Jerusalem (Luke 19:41) and prayed for those who crucified Him (Luke 23:34). Paul said his "heart's desire and prayer to God for the Israelites is that they may be saved" (Romans 10:1).

- Pray that God will help you make contact with those who are lost (Matthew 9:37,38).
- Pray that God will help you with the right attitude and the right approach to interest them in a study of His Word.
- Pray that the people you are working with can be drawn to Jesus (John 6:44).

- Pray that the people you are working with will seek to know God (Deuteronomy 4:29; Acts 17:27).
- Pray that the people you are working with will believe the Scriptures (Romans 10:17; 1 Thessalonians 2:13).
- Pray that the same people will be willing to give up all to follow Christ (2 Corinthians 5:15; Phillippians 3:7,8).

This book is based on the belief that Christians want congregational growth but are hampered by a faltering personal dedication and by a lack of leadership to know how to proceed. With new dedication, though, comes the need to locate prospects for Bible studies. To help with that problem, some facts from church growth research were mentioned in the last lesson. Those facts were:

(1) Several methods have proven more productive than cold canvassing.

(2) People that are being added to the membership rolls of growing churches are being reached through what is known as neighborhood Bible studies.

(3) One way for churches to grow is to find the hurt in the community and to heal it. People will thus be able to realize their deepest needs can be fulfilled only through becoming a Christian.

(4) Relationships are the major reason people eventually affiliate with a church.

Kent R. Hunter says that at least seven major occasions exist when people will be more open to Christians who desire to share the love of God and the good news of Jesus Christ with them.[1]

(1) When people first move into a community, they tend to be open to new things.

(2) When people are changing jobs or careers, whether they change residences or not, they are more open to change.

(3) People who have visited the church are more open than people who have not visited.

(4) Those who have been helped by the church are more open to an invitation to church services or a presentation of the good news of Jesus Christ.

(5) People who are friends of new members are often more receptive to the church.

(6) Economic difficulties tend to create a spiritual openness in people.

(7) Basic changes in society or milestones in history are also times when people are often more open to Christianity.

How Do You Do That?

How can these principles be implemented so Christians can win people like the church in Acts did? What would a business executive do if he had a tremendous product to sell and a large sales force, but no one came to his place of business asking to buy it? He would seek out people in the community in need of his product.

> What would a business executive do if he had a tremendous product to sell and a large sales force, but no one came to his place of business asking to buy it?

Like that businessman, Christians should locate the people in the community who have hurts or recognized needs and involve them in neighborhood Bible studies. The terms "hurts" or "recognized needs" does not necessarily indicate "problems." Problem people could be defined as alcoholics, the homeless, the jobless, drug addicts and those of similar nature. Cold, hard research and evangelism authorities say that people with such severe problems are usually the poorest prospects for conversion.

This is not to say that they should not be helped. It is to say that Christians should not build their entire evangelism program around people with devastating problems.

Every community and every congregation is different. People are different. What works in one community and in one congregation does not work exactly the same in a community a hundred miles away or half a nation away. If, however, certain general principles have been proven to work, the third application will surely show progress when adapted for use by a local congregation. If tactics have worked well in enough churches and enough situations, they bear consideration when your local evangelism plans are made. Here are a few suggestions for specific application.

Direct Mail

Any psychologist or counselor could pin-point the general needs of people in a community, but we then need to find those people and get them to identify themselves. One way to locate the people in the community who have hurts/needs would be through direct mail. Professionally prepared direct mail campaign pieces that are specifically prepared for this purpose are available. At the end of this lesson, information will be given on how you can obtain these as well as a mailing list of homes in your vicinity.

These have been prepared on a variety of themes and are designed to elicit a response from the recipient that will allow you to have an immediate contact with that person. Some of the subject areas covered by these direct mail pieces are:
- recovering from grief
- improving relationships
- divorce recovery
- parenting
- single parenting
- marriage relationships
- financial problems
- loneliness

Those who are interested in one of these topics will respond, which will allow you an opportunity to discuss the study with them. Although you make the initial contact, they are contacting you because of an expressed interest, providing evangelistic workers with open prospects who have a specific need.

Some workers do not even study the Bible with these people upon the first response. While full of Biblical applications, the studies or seminars are aimed at helping with specific needs within the community. The seminars are based on Biblical principles and present the thought that the

Bible alone has the answers for life. At the conclusion of these studies, an opportunity is offered for a Bible study.

I certainly would not hide the spiritual nature of the leader or congregation conducting the seminar, but not red flag it either. At this time, these people are not interested in a Bible study. They are interested in a class on how to be a better parent, how to be a better husband or wife, or one of several other relevant topics.

The purpose behind this is a three-step one. First, respondents are invited to participate in a good class on the subject of their interest. The class is taught by prepared individuals. After the first seminar has ended, class members will be invited (step two) to join an informal, nonthreatening Bible study with the same group. Eventually (step three) participants will be invited to a one-on-one indepth Bible study on how to become a Christian.

Most people are not sufficiently interested in studying the Bible to initially accept an invitation for that purpose. They are turned off at the idea of Bible studies until they are shown how relevant biblical principles are to their everyday problems.

A similar concept has been used in many parts of the world where advertisements for free classes to learn the English language produce numerous responses. The textbook used to teach these classes is the Bible. By this approach, they are able to teach English and to teach the Bible at the same time without objection from the students.

Most of the students probably would not have responded to an invitation to study the Bible. Through this kind of class, the teachers were able to identify those who had an interest in Bible study and were able to study more specifically with them individually.

In this same manner, people in your community will respond to an offer to enroll in a class on a subject in which they are interested. Church members teach the classes, and biblical principles are used as the basis for the class. In time, the prejudice of the students will be overcome through friendship with the teacher, and they may be willing to continue with more specific Bible studies.

Some people prefer to make the church connection very obvious up front. Although you may not get as large a crowd initially, you will not have high numbers dropping out later. The number of serious students this method produces is larger in the long run, its proponents feel.

Both methods can be used effectively. You should choose the method that you can participate in most comfortably.

Prior to distributing these mailing pieces, you will need to be prepared to conduct neighborhood studies. We recommend that each potential leader of these studies obtain and follow a good look that has been specifically prepared to help you conduct meaningful neighborhood studies even when you have had little or no experience.

> Multitudes of sincere people who are just waiting for someone to ask them to be part of any religious organization, and they will probably respond to the first invitation they get.

"Let's Talk"

Another means of finding people who want to learn more about the Bible is through a radio program called "Let's Talk." This program is presented by Glenn Owen in Abilene, Texas, and is distributed through the Herald of Truth. It enjoys a large listening audience wherever this radio program is broadcast.

"Let's Talk" is the only program of its kind, as far as I know. It is designed to produce contact with listeners that allows for personal follow-up contact. This is one of the program's objectives, and it achieves this goal naturally. Glenn's approach is to be able to eventually identify those listening who would be willing to study the Bible and to organize them into Bible study groups.

This program can be sponsored on a local radio station by a local church. After several years, Glenn is able to provide the local congregation with a number of people who would be receptive to neighborhood Bible studies. He does this by holding seminars in the area where the radio station is located.

Regular Bible Studies Would Appeal to Many

Before you come to the conclusion that the only people you will ever be able to teach are those with some kind of a problem, my experience is that many, ordinary people without special needs would welcome an opportunity to study the Bible. Some may be acquainted with the church of Christ and wonder what it stands for.

Many are not members of any church and for a variety of reasons will be open to talking about their religious status. Multitudes of sincere people are just waiting for someone to ask them to be part of any religious organization, and they will probably respond to the first invitation they get.

Some Christians will be able to persuade personal acquaintances or relatives to go through a study similar to what were once known as cottage Bible studies, another phrase for home Bible studies.

Youth Prime Evangelism Candidates

Youth is the ripest of all evangelistic fields. Those in their formative years are usually open and willing to consider new ideas, especially from their friends. They are idealistic enough to want truth and to accept it when they find it.

Christian teens and college students should be encouraged to be part of an aggressive evangelistic Bible study program. Young people do not have all of the hang-ups most adults must wrestle with, so they are able to bring their friends to church services and to converse with them about spiritual matters at length. Neither do their friends have the prejudices and apathy of older adults, so they are willing to study. This is a tremendous group that is only waiting on leadership.

Youth is the ripest of all evangelistic fields.

Teens respond well to relationships with other teens. You can always count on boys to come to church services or other youth activities if a girl invites them! Because teens have not developed any reason to turn down opportunities to go somewhere and do something, even if it is a church service, they will come if invited. Once a relationship has been created with the teen leader or others in the group, they can be quickly involved in a Bible study.

Have Others Set Up Studies for You

Many years ago, my wife sold Home Interior products; and from their practices, I learned a method we should be using in evangelism. When the Home Interior demonstrators held a show, they made it known that those attending could earn credits toward free products by booking a show in their home. They would get a certain amount of credit for booking and hosting the show, more credits for the number who came, and even more credits for the amount sold. After my wife's first show, she never again had to directly ask anyone to host a show. Those attending her shows voluntarily provided her with more bookings than she could handle.

We can use that same principle evangelistically. Many Christians do not feel they can teach a Bible study. But they have many friends who would be willing to set up studies and host them for those who are qualified to teach them. These people are a very definite part of the evangelism process.

We should take advantage of the zeal of new converts, just as the New Testament Christians did, by encouraging them to set up at least one Bible study with their friends or relatives. New converts usually are fired up and excited about the Good News and are anxious to share it. This also helps solidify their faith by immediately involving them in soul-winning. If a Bible teacher would ask each new convert to set up at least one study, he would never again lack students to teach.

Be Imaginative

The greatest uninspired book has not been written. The greatest speech has not been delivered. The most effective way to evangelize in our generation may not yet be conceived. The best way to find prospective students for home studies in our generation is yet to be designed.

We need to use our minds and be constantly working to improve methods and approaches. Something new and revolutionary is needed. What we have done in the past has not cured the ailment!

Let me give you some examples of what I mean by suggesting we be innovative in our evangelistic thinking. Several years ago, encyclopedia sales people went door-to-door selling their product. For more than one reason, they have ceased to do that but they have not gone out of business. They have, instead, changed their methods of finding prospects for their sales people.

You may have noticed that they have a booth at every type of show in all the convention centers and fairgrounds. At these booths, they have drawings and give away yardsticks and similar type gifts. Each one of the slips left in the drawing box will get a call from a salesperson in an attempt to set up an appointment for a sales presentation.

We must also become creative. For instance, in each city large enough to have shows of that nature, one area congregation could be responsible for renting the space and staffing a booth to find those who would like to have a home Bible study. This would mean that a really exciting display booth would need to be created and an excellent approach thought out for those stopping to investigate. Once an effective one was designed, similar ones could be used in every major city.

An integral part of this type of work has to be the follow-up after the contact. The failure of this type of work in many instances has been the lack of follow-through with those who indicated an interest in Bible study. This follow-up is even more important than the initial contact. The first contact and the whole idea of the exhibit is to be able to have this follow-up visit.

Daily, the mail brings letters offering a free item if the recipient will fill out and return an enclosed card. Odds are a salesman of some type will telephone to set up an appointment to bring the free gift and make a brief presentation concerning the product or service providing the gift.

A very nice letter could be sent to all the households in your congregation's region offering a free Bible with no obligation. When the cards are received, someone drops by the home to deliver the free Bible. From this contact, a Bible study might be a logical outcome.

Here is a sample letter used by a church in Chicago that was said to be so successful they had to stop sending it. The congregation could not respond to all the replies![2] It was used by a church in an area that contains predominantly apartment houses and condominiums.

Dear Friend:

If you are like most of us you probably don't mind making a new friend once in a while. Those of us who are neighbors in this area get pretty shut away from each other. Maybe you like it that way. But sometimes you may feel like sending out a test signal to see if anyone would even notice. I know I get that way occasionally.

Life is pretty much a sending out and receiving of signals, I guess. And when there isn't anybody around to listen—nobody "to tell it to"—a funny thing happens.

Maybe you know the "ghosts" that haunt your mind when it seems like nobody cares. Maybe you wrestle with anxieties—about your health, about your job, about your family, or some special friend. Maybe you wish there was somebody around to laugh with you, or to cry with you.

You'll have to overlook this kind of introduction by mail. What I would really like is to come and sit down in your living room. I'm just an ordinary man who happens to be the minister over at [insert your location or descriptive address here]. Don't let that scare you. I'm not asking you to join anything. I just thought you might like to know that I am here, and that I am available.

If you would like to make a new friend, here is one neighbor who would like to, too! You can let me know just by sending back the card I have enclosed. I'll be glad to stop by at your convenience.

Cordially yours,
[minister's name]

Marketing the Church

Christians must learn how to "market the church" if they are to convert the lost. This is a term you may have been

conditioned to dislike but it simply means to present something well. Some have mistakenly thought of marketing as
gimmicry and envisioned someone who has an ulterior desire to sell by deception.

Others are skeptical of connecting evangelism with any
mention of marketing or salesmanship, which they relate to
high pressure tactics. One author said:

> The Christianity which grows by careful market analysis and by
> careful attention to "what the consumers are buying" will lose its
> identity. Under these conditions it may grow when it has
> nothing left to say.[3]

> **Christians
> must learn how
> to "market the
> church" if they
> are to convert
> the lost.**

We cannot emphasize too
strongly that evangelism should
be built on a foundation of love
rather than gimmicks. There is no
place in biblical outreach for gimmicks, shallowness, manipulation, passing fads, quick fixes or
high pressure tactics.

As a young minister, I was very
active in home Bible studies. In
my enthusiasm, I trieid to do everything I could think of that
was scriptural and honest to baptize people.

I remember at one point trying to help people make a decision to be baptized. To do this, I would draw a line down
the middle of a sheet of paper, write "reasons for being baptized" at the top of one side, and "reasons for not being baptized" at the top of the other side. I had usually gone
through a series of five Bible studies by this time and felt
they needed to make a decision right then. I was also afraid
that if they put off a decision until later, they might never
make it.

As I matured in my experience, I no longer use this rather
high-pressure gimmick. All of us have learned that certain
approaches done in conscientiousness and zeal did not
achieve what we wanted accomplished.

Positioning ourselves for evangelism, however, means
that we take wisdom from many disciplines and use it to
spread the gospel more effectively. For instance, we have
learned that printing in color with good design and lots of

illustrations on good quality paper is evangelistically more effective than lots of words printed in black on a page. We learned this from advertising experts.

We also know that using illustrations, repetition, visuals and discussion helps students retain what we teach about the Bible. We learned that from secular education.

A Lesson from a Peanut

We need to recognize what is counter-productive as well as what is useful and helpful from any discipline. We then treat that as we would a peanut—eat the nourishing nut and throw away the shell.

Marketing is a serious and thoughtful process. Marketing is what you do to promote and make your product look its best. It involves studying people, their needs and their receptivity.

When we talk about marketing the church, we are not talking about changing the gospel or compromising it in any way. To market the church means that we will study individuals, groups and communities in order to communicate the gospel more directly, powerfully and effectively. In modern terminology, we are "packaging the truth," which means that we are trying to show that Christianity is practical and contemporary and acceptable.

Jesus was "marketing the church" when He, and later the apostles, reinforced His teaching with miracles. The more we learn about marketing and applying it to evangelism, the more effective soul-winners we will be.

Our real competition today is in marketing—not in denominational groups. The competition for Christianity is from organizations, opportunities and philosophies that provide people with an alternative to the Christian life.

Our main competition is ABC, CBS, Universal Studios, MGN, K-Mart, JC Penny, etc. These organizations continually and aggressively seek to place their products, services and philosophies at the core of the lives of the same people the church is trying to reach. They are highly sophisticated marketers, driven by precise goals and objectives.

The more Christians know about how secular companies,

such as those mentioned above, succeed, the more we can adapt their successful methods to spreading the gospel and saving souls. The principles involved in selling goods and soul-winning are essentially the same. *We just have a better product!*

Do What Works

For many of you, no suggestions need to be made about how to go about developing and implementing Bible studies aimed at converting people. You just need to be encouraged to begin immediately and to persist. Bible studies can be set up and conducted in lots of ways. I would encourage you to use anything that works for you. Our objective is to win souls and to keep them saved. If there is a way that this objective can be scripturally accomplished, it should be used.

A man was in an engineering class in which one of the projects was to determine the height of a certain tall building. He was supposed to use a barometer to determine this, but he did not know how to use this instrument. So he decided he would find the answer some other way. He went to the top of the building and tied a weight on the end of a long string. He then let the string over the side of the building until it reached the ground and measured how long the string was. His teacher said he had the right answer but refused to accept it because he had solved the problem incorrectly.

His next approach was to go to the superintendent of the building and offer to give him the barometer if he would tell him the height of the building. Again he got the correct answer, but his teacher would not accept it because he had not obtained it correctly.

In converting the lost, we are not bound by such stringent rules. Whatever method that is right in itself and accomplishes the objective is acceptable to God.

Many souls have been saved through an evangelism program that works for one individual but not for another. A young boy in Missouri—standing shoulder to shoulder with experienced fishermen—caught a 15 lb. 6 oz. trout with a throw line and an oversized hook. His bait was a piece of lye soap, a french fry and a piece of napkin. But you cannot argue with success.

Sneak Preview

Just knowing how to identify potential Bible study prospects and knowing how to teach the plan of salvation does not make a congregation grow. Important ingredients are yet to be considered. They will be added to the game plan in the next chapter.

Discussion Starters

1. Without being concerned about money, "brainstorm" ideas, any ideas, that might get us in contact with people in our community.
2. What would a business do if no one came to them to buy their product?
3. Do you see any "marketing" or "packaging" concepts in the New Testament? If so, discuss them.
4. List some needs in your community and consider how the gospel could be packaged to respond to this need.

RESPONSE TO THIS CHAPTER

1. For me, the most meaningful part of chapter eight is

_____

_____

Why?

_____

2. One thing in chapter eight I do not understand is

_____

_____

113

3. One thing I do not agree with in this chapter is

_____

_____

Why?

_____

4. The one point in this chapter I wish our group could discuss further is

_____

_____

5. Other reactions I have to this chapter are

_____

_____

The following sources offer direct mail information, information services and mailing lists. Call or write for information on what they offer to verify that it is what you are looking for.

Dataman Information Services, Inc.
1100 Johnson Ferry Rd. NE
Suite 450
Atlanta, GA 30342

Walter Mueller
Specialized Ministries Center
855 Welsh Road
Maple Glen, PA 19002

Church Information and Development Services
3001 Redhill Ave.
Suite 2-220
Costa Mesa, CA 92626
(714) 957-1282

Reaching the Newcomer
P. O. Box 640
Grapevine, TX 76051

For more information about *Let's Talk* contact:

Glenn Owen
Let's Talk
P. O. Box 200
Abilene, TX 79604

Notes

1. Kent R. Hunter. *Moving the Church Into Action* (St. Louis: Concordia, 1989), pp. 129-130.
2. Taken from *How to Create a Direct Mail Campaign*. Specialized Ministries Center, 855 Welsh Road, Maple Glen, PA 19002.
3. James Thompson. The Church in Exile (Abilene, TX: ACU Press, 1990), p. 48.

Part 5

DECISIVE
COMMITMENT

*Who Will Pay
for the Hole in the Roof?*

9 WHAT PRICE EVANGELISTIC SUCCESS?

The Qualities Necessary For A Congregation to Succeed

CHAPTER HIGHLIGHTS

* Everyone of Us Can Do Something
* "Ninety Percent of Evangelism is Love"
* Effective Soul Winning Demands the Planning of Great Programs and the Attempting of Great Goals
* The Lord Wants His People to Dream Big Dreams
* There Is No Effortless Way to Reach the Lost
* The Church In Our Generation Can Live up to Christ's Expectations

Anyone contemplating a career as a basketball player should realistically assess his chance for success. Height and natural athletic ability would be primary requirements. Some have been successful in playing basketball who were not tall, but these people are exceptions. A short person has about as much chance of becoming a professional basketball player today as he does of swimming from Miami to Nassau. Those who are tall and have some native athletic ability have far greater opportunities to succeed in the basketball world.

Similarly, before a congregation starts a program of evangelism, they should determine what has to be done in order to succeed. Certain qualities are absolutely essential for a congregation to succeed in having a successful disciple making program.

The good news about these qualities is that anybody can develop them, if they want to. Unlike the basketball player who must rely on genes for both height and innate ability, the traits a Christian needs for successful soul winning can be developed. And, if a congregation does not develop these traits then it does not convert the lost. These attitudes must characterize both the leaders and the members.

Begin With Repentance

First, consider the quality of repentance.

Positioning a church for ongoing evangelism goes far beyond implementing a program or hiring additional staff. Ultimately, it takes a corporate change of heart.[1]

If a congregation has not been growing, then it means the members have not been personally teaching the lost; and that means the commandments of the Lord have been neglected. In spite of a command to teach and convert, the lost have been ignored. Individual Christians have not been distressed about congregational lack of growth. Instead they have been selfishly serving only themselves.

Soul-winning was the priority of Jesus and has to become the priority of each Christian. Each Christian must accept personal responsibility for finding and teaching the lost. "I'm responsible" should become the admission and battle cry of each of us. The words should be put on bulletin boards and made into badges. People may be curious enough to ask "Responsible for what."

Each individual member must come to the conclusion that there is something he can and should be doing about the lost. Perhaps some will teach Bible studies, others will set up the studies and host them in their homes, and some may babysit for those who are teaching. Others may help in dozens of varied ways that only local needs will spotlight. But there is something that each individual Christian can do.

Leaders Must Lead

No program can succeed without the right type of leadership. The leaders of a soul-winning program must have developed a high degree of personal spirituality. The congregation needs to see an example of concern that reflects an overwhelming committment to reach and save the lost.

Love

Love must be our supreme motivation. It encourages people to do what is right and then sustains them for the long haul. Loving the lost requires a commitment to give of ourselves, our energy and our money to do whatever it takes to reach and teach lost souls. Bob Smith said, "Ninety percent of evangelism is love."

Faith

Lack of faith has sabotaged many evangelism programs. Effective and successful soul-winning demands the planning of remarkable programs and the implementation of great works. This requires faith.

Satan has strewn many obstacles along the pathway. He has planted the prickly barbed wire of self doubt, the mine fields of procrastination, and the nuclear bomb of self-imposed biblical ignorance. Evangelism requires a lot of work, a lot of money and a lot of faith.

Clayton Pepper, a Nashville minister, has figured that the cost of personal evangelism programs is roughly $3.50 per convert. Church growth experts recommend that at least $1 out of every $10 in a congregation's income should be budgeted for evangelism. If evangelizing the lost is a priority, the congregation should be prepared to pay cost.

On occasion, solutions to obstacles in the way of growth may not be apparent, but a faith in God still calls for full steam ahead. If a congregation is doing His will, then faith assures that He will bless the group's efforts with success. But those who do not have a dynamic faith will never grow and never convert the lost.

Hard Work

A very enlightening phrase is found in 1 Corinthians 15:58.

> Therefore, my dear brothers, stand firm. Let nothing move you. Always give yourselves fully to the work of the Lord, because you know that your labor in the Lord is not in vain.

That phrase, "Always give yourselves fully to the work of the Lord," means to work hard at it. Good works succeed because some people are really working. On the other hand, many evangelistic programs fail because so few are working.

A church wag has observed that most church members today have been sitting so long they have "ingrown shirttails." The only way to change this is to declare war on laziness and indifference. A Christian must give himself to the harvest of souls with renewed enthusiasm and tireless labor. Winston Churchill said, "Most of the significant contributions that have been made to society have been made by people who were tired."[2] Success requires hard work. The lost cannot be saved while all the Christians are at home sitting in their dens reading the newspaper and watching television.

Prayer

If a Christian believes the teachings of the Bible, he will ask God for the tools needed to accomplish His work. This obvious point sometimes gets overlooked. If God commanded that something be done, He wants Christians to pray about it. Christians should ask for help in finding receptive hearts to teach. As individuals and as a church, praying for success in converting the lost should always be a high priority.

The Lord specifically taught His disciples to pray for harvesters (Matthew 9:37,38). Pray, also, that the Lord will use each member of your congregation. Pray for an increased passion for the lost, for opportunities to teach, and especially for the courage and faith to seize the opportunities as they come.

Vision

Asked to describe his wife's cooking, one old farmer answered: "It's fantastically adequate."

Many congregations are like the farmer's wife's cooking. They cannot envision anything greater than mediocre. But the Lord wants His people to dream big dreams for Him, to visualize great accomplishments for Him. He wants Christians to ask Him for big things. Christians should be a people who are not afraid to set goals and who are willing to sacrifice to accomplish their visions.

From the Great Commission and the accomplishments of the early church in the book of Acts, we know that God has always expected—even today—the church to set its sights on big things. For a congregation to be too content and its exertions too languid is a sin.

Christians need to be willing to take risks to extend themselves past their comfort zones, and to be willing to do more than just take the safe route. Leaders who are afraid of failure will not take the risks necessary to grow. Taking risks is called faith.

Sacrifice

Another key to acceptable and pleasing service for God is given in Romans 12:1.

Therefore, I urge you, brothers, in view of God's mercy, *to offer your bodies as living sacrifices,* holy and pleasing to God—which is your spiritual worship.

There is no effortless way to reach lost people. God's children must be ready and willing to give up part of their leisure time to teach. We must be willing to dig into our pockets to pay for the necessary resources and materials.

Each person must give of himself or herself as a slave of Jesus Christ. The attitude collectively and individually, must be that each is willing to do whatever it takes to reach and teach the lost.

One congregation started a successful bus program by purchasing 26 buses, each costing $3,000. What is outstanding is that those buses were bought and paid for by individual members.

> No program can succeed without the right kind of leadership.

Widows were working in order to make the payments on buses they had given. One young man sold his car to buy a bus for the program.

One 91-year-old man bought a bus with the money that he had saved to pay for his funeral. He reasoned that he could save that much money again in seven years. At his age, he doubted that he would live much longer than another seven years, anyway. Sacrifice! These examples seem to describe the type of sacrifice Paul wrote about in Romans.

A well-known saying in America is that there ain't no free lunch. Neither is evangelism free.

Determination

Four men once brought a paralyzed friend to see Jesus. They knew Christ would heal him, but they could not get near enough because of the crowd. Undaunted, they dragged their friend onto the roof of the house and proceeded to tear a hole in the roof. They then lowered the paralyzed one to Jesus' feet.

Jesus was impressed with that. Here were men so dedicated to saving a friend that they tore a hole in the roof. No doubt they later had to fix the roof, but they cared enough to pay the cost.

The personal worker's attitude is one of determination. He looks at every program in light of soul-winning. He eats, drinks, thinks and sleeps soul winning. The determination of a fullback with the ball on the one-yard line is nothing compared to a committed soul winner!

He is so dedicated that he is willing to work as long as necessary to succeed. He knows that it may take several years to see the effects of his labor. He realizes that attitudes are not changed overnight. He is prepared to tear a hole in the roof, if necessary.

Hearts on Fire

Probably more than 95% of the members of most congregations have never influenced anyone outside of their own children to become a Christian. Yet the first and greatest passion of Jesus was to "seek and save the lost."

To follow the example of Jesus, we cannot be satisfied with the status quo. We must believe something effective can be done to convert people. The church can, in this generation, be everything Christ wanted it to be. It can and must recapture the fervor of those early founding years. The dedicated Christian will settle for nothing less regardless of what it costs.

"Ninety percent of evangelism is love."

As a church growth consultant, Wayne McDill says he has observed four levels of outreach thinking in churches.

First is the **verbal** level when outreach is given empty lip service in the context of a maintenance mentality. Second is the **promotional** level where outreach is pushed as a survival necessity for the congregation. The third is the **commitment** level where church leaders have genuine desire to reach people and, therefore, give priority to evangelism in the planning, programming, and worship of the church.

The fourth level is the **overflow** level when the vitality and meaning of church life results in an enthusiastic outreach by members and a magnetic attraction to outsiders. . . .

The churches expressing an **overflow** level of outreach thinking seem to transcend normal planning and programming and move into a different dimension of effectiveness. Evangelism just seems to happen. It seems as normal as breathing for the body. It is an expression of life and health, a vital sign of unmistakable spiritual strength. In every church I have seen experience this overflow, the relational approach to evangelism was stressed. But beneath the apparent spontaneity was careful planning, praying, and action by church leaders.[3]

An evangelistic program needs to develop into a lifestyle to be really effective. Disciple making needs to be happening even if a leader is not calling meetings and cranking up a program.

An "outreach program" probably didn't exist in the New Testament congregations. Those early-day Christians carried a natural burden on their hearts for the lost.

If today's hearts carried a similar burden, then the church would still save the lost without a program. However, there will always be a place nd a need for selecting and training "fishers of men" like Jesus did the twelve.

> . . . praying for success in converting the lost should always be a high priority.

Decisive Commitment

The Romans are said to have once invaded the British Isles at the cliffs of Dover. The first time they attacked, they were repulsed. For their second attack, the British outnumbered them three to one. However, the Roman army returned, took supplies ashore, and burned their boats behind them. Then they unsheathed their swords and marched with forceful resolution into battle. Such total commitment was so unimaginable to the British that the Romans were victorious.

When Christians learn that kind of total commitment to the cause of Christ, they will also be victorious.

Sneak Preview

One of the three great enemies of evangelism has not been discussed. We have left it for last. This great killer of evangelistic commitment is called "fear," and we will tackle it in the last chapter.

DISCUSSION STARTERS

1. Do you feel the need for repentance as an individual because of your lack of effort to convert people?
2. Do you feel the need for repentance as a congregation because of the lack of emphasis on personal evangelism?
3. Why do we have trouble making evangelism a top priority in our lives?
4. What do you feel are the top three qualities necessary for evangelistic success in your own life? For your congregation?
5. Briefly discuss the importance of each character trait mentioned. Which do you personally most need to strengthen?
6. Why do you think Jesus was so impressed by the act of lowering the man through the hole in the roof? What kind of "holes in roofs" might we have to make?

RESPONSE TO THIS CHAPTER

1. For me, the most meaningful part of chapter nine is

_____

_____

Why?

_____

2. One thing in chapter nine I do not understand is

_____

_____

3. One thing I do not agree with in this chapter is

_____

_____

   Why?

_____

4. The one point in this chapter I wish our group could discuss further is

_____

_____

5. Other reactions I have to this chapter are

_____

_____

Notes

1. Calvin Ratz, *Mastering Outreach & Evangelism* (Portland: Multnomah, 1990), p. 50.
2. Paul W. Powell, *Go-Givers in a Go-Getter World* (Nashville: Broadman Press, 1986). p. 31.
3. Wayne McDill, *Making Friends for Christ* (Nashville: Broadman Press, 1979), p. 119.

Part 5: DECISIVE COMMITMENT

10 ARE YOU AFRAID OF THE DARK?

Eliminating Imaginary Fears

CHAPTER HIGHLIGHTS

* Personal Evangelism Can Be A Terrifying Experience
* Turning Fear into Energy
* The Three Kinds of Fear
* Common But Unrealistic Anxieties
* Jesus Also Failed
* The Word's Power to Overcome Fear
* Our Confidence is in the Message
* God Will Give the Increase

People do not involve themselves in an evangelistic outreach for several major reasons. As I see them, the reasons are:

(1) Lack of leadership
(2) Indifference or lack of commitment
(3) Fear

An attempt at direct personal evangelism is a terrifying

129

experience for some novice teachers. Their fear is almost un-controllable and is the primary reason people abandon per-sonal work.

A Christian is either overcome with the fear of change—what he will have to do to become a soul winner—or he succumbs to the fear of rejection. But as Franklin Delano Roosevelt said at the height of World War II: "We have nothing to fear but fear itself."

Timidity has kept many a Christian from never making an attempt to do any kind of visitation or evangelism. Someone described what happens by saying, "My mind goes blank, my palms get sweaty, and nothing I say seems to make any sense."

Lining Up Your Butterflies

Being apprehensive about trying to teach someone the Bi-ble is not a sin. As a matter of fact, having some fear is help-ful and will keep us alert and prayerful.

Public speaking makes many people very nervous; for some people it is the most debilitating thing they will ever be asked to do. But all experienced public speakers realize that some nervousness is good because it keeps them on their toes, compels them to prepare well, and helps fuel the extra effort to make sure all goes well. The old saying among pub-lic speakers is that having butterflies in your stomach is not bad, as long as you make them fly in formation.

Our vivid imaginations make it hard for us to tell the dif-ference between real and unreal fears. People experience just as much fear of what they think might be in the darkness as they experience when confronted by a real threat.

Most fears that accompany evangelism efforts can be elim-inated through training and experience because they are un-realistic and imaginary. These fears need to be isolated and then conquered or else they will cripple our effectiveness.

Overcoming a fearful attitude is not as difficult as gener-ally believed if a person wants to overcome his problems. Trying to evangelize the unconverted usually involves three kinds of fear.

A Sense of Inadequacy

Common to most is feeling that we do not have the basic talent to set up Bible studies and to teach non-Christians. We think we will not know what to say, that we do not have the skills needed to do this kind of work, and that we cannot answer the questions our students might ask. We fear we do not know the Bible well enough to be attempting this.

Regular personal Bible study will help alleviate this fear. Serving as an assistant to an accomplished teacher also helps considerably. Besides removing the mystery that surrounds teaching, a novice quickly learns that preparation, not natural talent has equipped his teacher.

A more subtle development also occurs as the novice begins to take part in the class. After all, the teacher is probably an old friend, someone the novice teacher had always considered an equal in the Lord's church. Seeing someone we know accomplish with ease what we were afraid to do can help us feel more courageous.

Veteran workers should always be trying to train others. You will be surprised at how quickly this helps to allay fears.

> Most fears that accompany evangelism efforts can be eliminated through training and experience because they are unrealistic and imaginary.

Fear of Rejection.

I worked my way through college selling Bibles door-to-door in the summertime. At the time, I was young and very shy and hated calling on strangers. I was so shy that, in the small town where I lived, I would cross to the other side of the street rather than speak to a person coming my way on the sidewalk. And here I was selling door-to-door! It particularly bothered me when someone was rude or slammed the door in my face.

When several of us got together later and shared our experiences, I could relate to the young man who told of driving around the block several times each morning before finally stopping and going up to the first door. Then he would knock very lightly, hoping no one would be home.

We had those feelings because we feared rejection. Finally, experience taught me that any adverse reactions by homeowners did not represent their attitude toward my personality, my appearance or even my ability. Some of those homeowners would have approached the door with a scowl of rejection if I had been standing there with a million dollars for them. But, we were taking their rejection personally, and this was a mistake that was affecting our attitudes toward our work and our sales.

Fortunately, I did overcome the fear of rejection, but I have had an abiding sympathy ever since for fellow Christians who suffer like fears. No one likes to be turned down. And when working in evangelism, it is easy to believe that people may not like our attempts to influence them, especially about things religious.

We are afraid they will think we are "religious nuts." We are afraid of being different.

Another cause for rejection is the subject itself. When a non-Christian hears the pure gospel for the first time, he has to deal with the very depths of his existence.

If reared in a denomination, he must deal with his forefathers. "If it's good enough for mom and dad, it's good enough for me." He has to deal with the current state of his own soul and those he loves. "You trying to tell me that a good person won't go to heaven?"

He has to counter years of teaching or assumptions that the simple gospel will challenge. The easiest way for him to deal with all this is to simply reject the new message and reject the person who bears the message.

Fear of Failure.

When making our first attempts to call on prospective Christians, we can think of so many ways in which we might fail. They may refuse our request for an opportunity to study with them. Or we can complete a study but they will not be interested in making a decision to live for Christ. Maybe we won't be able to answer their questions, or they might disagree with what we say.

Again we have a tendency to take all of this personally. If they reject our message, we feel we have failed. Remember that many people also rejected Christ's message. It helps to know He understands how we feel.

These three kinds of anxieties are common for the beginning evangelistic worker. Later on in our lives, we will look back at those things and laugh at them as Paul Little did when he tells about his first attempts to evangelize.

> About every six months the pressure to witness used to reach explosive heights inside me. Not knowing any better, I would suddenly lunge at someone and spout all my verses with a sort of glazed stare in my eye. I honestly didn't expect any response. As soon as my victim indicated lack of interest, I'd begin to edge away from him with a sign of relief and the consoling thought, "All that will live godly in Christ Jesus shall suffer persecution" (2 Timothy 3:12).[1]

These kinds of feelings are nothing new, and everyone has them. But they are unrealistic. To continue to have them is harmful and will hinder us from doing God's work.

Even Jesus Failed

We do not need to fear failure. We will fail to set up studies or to convert people many times. We need to face that fact.

Jesus failed many times. Isaiah 53:3 prophecied that Jesus would be despised and rejected. He was, and still is, rejected by the Jews. But that is no reflection on Jesus!

Jesus failed to convert the rich young ruler in Matthew 19:16-30. Jesus said everything right, and He said it in the right way, but the young man left without be-

> . . . our confidence in evangelism is in the product, the biblical message, not in our own ability.

coming a follower. The fault was not in the teacher but in the man who rejected the message and person of Jesus.

The parable of the soils and the sower (Matthew 13:1-23) teaches that our messages will be heard by four kinds of soil or hearts. Jesus said that only one of those four kinds will accept the message, act upon it and bear fruit for the Lord. This is not teaching that only one out of every four hearers will respond favorably, but it does teach that many will not receive the Word positively. The problem is not in the message or the presentation of the message, but in the heart of the hearer.

Pray for Boldness

Fearful souls are in good company. Paul said he "came...in weakness and fear, and with much trembling" (1 Corinthians 2:3). He also asked the Ephesian brethren:

> Pray also for me, that whenever I open my mouth, words may be given me so that I will fearlessly make known the mystery of the gospel, for which I am an ambassador in chains. Pray that I may declare it fearlessly, as I should (Ephesians 6:19,20).

The first recorded prayer of Jerusalem Christians was for boldness. Peter and John had just been released after being imprisoned for preaching the gospel. Their prayer was not to eliminate their enemies but that they might have the courage to face the danger. We have the same God to whom they were praying. He will answer our prayer for boldness as He answered theirs.

I suspect that this matter of fear was one of the reasons Jesus sent the seventy and the twelve out to teach in teams of two. Two can bolster each other and help vanquish fear.

Paul Cautioned Timothy Against Fear

Evidently Timothy was bothered by some of the same kinds of fear we have because Paul reminded him of a fact important to any Christian who takes his responsibility to Christ seriously.

For God did not give us a spirit of timidity, but a spirit of power, of love and of self-discipline. So do not be ashamed to testify about our Lord, or ashamed of me his prisoner. But join with me in suffering for the gospel, by the power of God (2 Timothy 1:7,8).

Paul is reminding Timothy and us that the cure for being timid is the realization we have power, love and self-discipline.

We have the power of God working for us when we are trying to teach non-Christians. Our real strength is the Word of God. When we are teaching the Bible, we do not have to worry about how persuasive we are or if we can answer all of a person's arguments or objections. The Bible is powerful enough that it will work on their hearts. That relieves us of the burden.

Loving people and wanting them to be saved is also a strong antidote for timidity. If your love for people is strong, your fear of talking to them will soon be overcome by your concern for them.

How does self-discipline help us? People who are lost will not be saved without your message from God. A Christian may have fears of inadequacy, of failure and of rejection, but he knows he must discipline himself to go to the lost with this powerful soul-saving message anyway.

An obese person does not give up eating fattening foods because he has lost his taste for them; instead, he disciplines himself to do without because he knows those foods will cause health problems.

We may be afraid of the dark, but we discipline ourselves to go check out a bump in the night. It may be with fear and trembling, but we go because the alternative is unacceptable to us. Eventually we come to realize that these fears are more imagination than reality. It soon is no big deal to go turn on the light and check on a noise to discover that we only left the cat in.

Here's the Answer

First, it is good for us to have weaknesses. Read Paul's discovery concerning his weak points:

> But he said to me, "My grace is sufficient for you, for my power is made perfect in weakness." Therefore I will boast all the more gladly about my weaknesses, so that Christ's power may rest on me. That is why, for Christ's sake, I delight in weaknesses, in insults, in hardships, in persecutions, in difficulties. For when I am weak, then I am strong (2 Corinthians 12:9,10).

Paul's meaning is that having weaknesses makes us rely on Christ and His ability to achieve through us, rather than on our own strength to get the task done. From this vantage point, being weak is better than being strong. The weak person depends on God, which is what God wants. The person who believes himself to be strong does not feel as much need for God.

Second, we can overcome our fears and timidity by realizing our confidence in evangelism is in the product, the biblical message, not in our own ability. We must remove ourselves from the picture and quit focusing on our own feeble power.

If we take the emphasis away from the presenter (us) and place it on the message being presented, we will be relying on God. God will then be free to work His power in the lives of those people.

An attitude of fear is not consistent with the resources God has given us. The only effective way to defeat fear is a faith and confidence in God to work through us. Not only will this neutralize our fear but it will eventually banish it completely.

Third, if we are right in what we are doing and saying, and people refuse to hear or obey the message, they are wrong, not us. We have won the battle because we tried. God asks of us faithfulness, not success. The burden for success is on God; He has taken that for Himself. Our burden is simply to do our best to fulfill the responsibility God has given us, which is to preach the gospel.

> The burden for success is on God; He has taken that for Himself.

Success for our endeavors will definitely come. But the emphasis in our responsibility is to preach and teach. God will give the increase. The increase of the Kingdom is a responsibility He has reserved for Himself.

Again, 1 Corinthians 3:6-9 is an important lesson for us to learn in relation to this problem.

> I planted the seed, Apollos watered it, but God made it grow. So neither he who plants nor he who waters is anything, but only God, who makes things grow. The man who plants and the man who waters have one purpose, and each will be rewarded according to his own labor. For we are God's fellow workers; you are God's field, God's building.

If you have a Bible study and do not convert the people, what is God saying here about that? The lesson is that sometimes we are only part of the process of conversion. What we have done is plant the seed. Maybe the seed dies and nothing ever comes of our work. On the other hand, maybe we have softened the soil for the next Christian who tries to influence them.

One person plants the seed and another comes along and waters. But do not ever forget that God will give the increase. God's Word will act upon that heart—if the person will let it.

Fourth, we can find help among our brothers and sisters in the family of God. I have known a few people who could literally set up Bible studies walking down the street. Some of them were also great teachers. Some were not, but they could keep several teachers busy.

One man could go into a restaurant and build a warm relationship with the waitress before she had even taken his order. And before lunch was over, he would have done something to share his faith with her.

If you are fortunate enough to know someone like that, do your best to spend as much time with them as you can. Try to determine what personality traits they possess that allow them to succeed. Even if you are never as successful as they are, just being around them will give you a lot of confidence.

Another very helpful thing to do is to organize the personal evangelism workers in the congregation into a support group. Hold meetings at appropriate times and discuss the successes and problems each of you are experiencing. In that meeting, spend some time brain storming about how to handle problems. You will be amazed at the great ideas and super encouragement that will come out of such meetings. And don't forget the value of Christians praying over problems and asking God for solutions (James 5:16).

The Courage of Conviction

You know that what you are doing is right. It must be done if the lost are to be saved. Because of that, you will find a way to handle any problems. God will bless you as is taught in the parable of the talents.

To overcome the fear we all experience when approaching someone with the Gospel, we must have the conviction that God has given us a message that people desperately need to hear. This kind of conviction will free us from fear.

A young man walking down the street notices a building on fire. The automobiles parked outside are mute testimony that the building is full of people. He immediately rushes in screaming "Fire! Fire!" The young man had no fear of rejection, no hesitation to scream the message. Why? Because he knew the people needed to hear what he had to tell them.

Look Into the Future

A great way to handle timidity is to look past that fearful beginning to the time when a family you are teaching becomes Christians. Because of your part in their salvation, they will always feel that you are one of their closest friends. The feeling between an evangelist and those he has taught the truth is special—a closeness that comes only with this relationship.

Learn to see souls rather than bodies, and learn to love those souls. Realize that a couple that has been converted will produce Christian children who will marry and produce more Christian children.

This cycle will go on and on, all because Christ died for our sins, and that sacrifice, which made possible eternal salvation, caused your heart to be on fire.

Discussion Starters

1. What are you most afraid of? Heights? Close places? Snakes? How do you handle this fear?
2. What part has fear played in your own attempts at evangelism?
3. Have you ever found yourself in a situation where fear of failure, rejection or inadequacy made you hesitate to do something that needed to be done? When? What did you do?
4. If you do not experience shyness with strangers, explain to the class how you have managed to achieve this.
5. What does it mean that our confidence is in the biblical message?
6. Have you known a person who "never met a stranger" and could set up Bible studies anywhere? If so, analyze what about that person gave them that ability?

RESPONSE TO THIS CHAPTER

1. For me, the most meaningful part of chapter ten is

_____

_____

Why?

_____

2. One thing in chapter ten I do not understand is

_____

_____

3. One thing I do not agree with in this chapter is

_____

_____

Why?

_____

4. The one point in this chapter I wish our group could discuss further is

_____

_____

5. Other reactions I have to this chapter are

_____

_____

Notes

1. Paul E. Little, *How to Give Away Your Faith* (Downers Grove, Illinois: Inter-Varsity Press, 1966), p. 32.

Epilogue

Paul, Kathy and the Central Church

Divine providence? You could not convince Paul and Kathy Stewart that it was otherwise.

Only a few days after their late-night soul-searching, a letter came from missionaries the church supported in Mexico City. Bryan and Peggy Norman had requested that the church send someone to work with them for a month.

"It might give you some idea what missionary work is like," Bryan had written. "And it would allow someone to make a personal report."

The Normans went on to offer lodging "and plenty of personal work."

Kathy spotted the letter pinned to the bulletin board. It became their dinner table topic.

"But for a month?" Sixteen-year-old Paul Jr. was not so sure that he could be that long without junk food, television and rock music.

"I think it would be neat," was six-year-old Julie's thought. She knew that life would be grand anywhere as long as her parents were there.

But it was 13-year-old Jim who put it into perspective.

"Wouldn't it be great to teach someone and see them baptized?"

It took some effort, but Paul arranged a month's leave of absence. The trip was scheduled during the summer months. Now they had returned, and Paul stood before the Central congregation. Paul Jr. and Jim flanked him. He felt pride bursting in him.

These boys had never spoken to a congregation, but they would be part of this report. How they had grown spiritually over the past four weeks! Jim was now talking about becoming a preacher—perhaps a missionary, and Paul Jr. was beginning to discern between worldly and Biblical ways.

141

Paul had not realized before how far his son had wandered from things spiritual. He was not a rebellious youth; he had just been weak spiritually.

Heavenly Father, give me the right words to help your people here understand the challenge—that the harvest is indeed plentiful, not only in a foreign country, but here.

"I have just returned from the greatest life-changing experience I have ever known," Paul began. "As most of you know, my family spent a month with Bryan and Peggy Norman, one of our missionary families."

"We went to encourage them in their mission and to help them preach the gospel under difficult circumstances," he began, glancing around at the large building and the comfortable seats. He was remembering the small homes crowded with people, the meager meals, the Bible being read by lamplight.

"What I didn't realize when I left was that this experience was going to change our lives.

"When I saw how hard the Normans worked and the intensity with which Bryan preached, I came to experience shame for the meager efforts I have been exerting.

"I saw the joy in the lives of those who were converted! I rejoiced with them as they brought others to hear about this Jesus to whom they had committed their lives."

Am I reaching these people? He looked at the Smiths. Joe was nodding off as he did every week; Rachel was cleaning her fingernails. Their children were passing notes.

The Jones were no different. John was busy reading the bulletin while Mary stared intently into Paul's face. She wanted to know more. The Whites were whispering. For the first time, Paul experienced a frustration he had never known.

He slammed his hand onto the pulpit, the crack resounding throughout the building. Heads snapped up, whispers ceased, pencils stopped moving.

"Now that I've got everyone's attention, I want to ask you to really listen to me. Please take a few minutes because this is very important," he said. "I'm trying to get a point across that can save our souls, the souls of others, and perhaps help this church grow.

"In the beginning, I rationalized that this was happening because we were in a foreign country. Then I realized that people are people wherever they live and whatever language they speak.

"They didn't use the same methods we have tried with very little success in the United States. I lay awake at night trying to explain these things. I had always assumed that if we preached the gospel in our church buildings, the lost would come and hear it if they were interested. I had also come to the conclusion that most people in this materialistic age were no longer interested in the Christian life.

"I haven't personally taught anyone in years! I thought of that when I realized the congregation in that mission area is only five years old but already larger than this congregation.

"Those new Christians in that backward country were excited about their new faith and excited about sharing it with others. Some of those men were going to nearby areas to preach on Sundays when they had only been Christians themselves a little over a year. I met some of the most loving brothers and sisters you could ever know and later learned how much change had occurred in their lives since their conversion.

"One long night Kathy and I hardly slept as we came to realize that the gospel has not lost its power. The same thing could occur right here in Central!

"I am not the same person I was when I left a month ago. My family is not the same. We are going to be different," he said. "From this day forward I am going to be a soul-winner for Jesus. I apologize to you and to God for my former lackadaisical, uncaring example."

Paul's sermon was the talk of the congregation. The Smiths, the Jones and the Whites could not help but discuss it at their dinner tables. While Paul had been adamant, even forceful, his obvious love of souls had shown through. And the boys! Their change had been beyond belief. You could feel a change sweeping the congregation. It was an exciting time.

The next Sunday, each elder spoke to the congregation. They had met many times during the past week.

"We have decided that we have been part of the problem,"

brother Bill Davis said in speaking for the group. "We have agonized for several years over the nongrowth of the Central church.

"Now that we recognize the problem, we're going to make some changes, the first being that this congregation will become evangelistic," he said.

For the first time in years, the members did not rush outdoors and into their automobiles at the final "Amen." The people could feel a new energy, a new life and attitude that was beginning to permeate the congregation. The Smiths stayed to visit. The Jones asked them to come over Monday night.

"Let's have a prayer meeting about this," John Jones suggested, surprised at himself.

"How do you do that? I've never been to a prayer meeting," Joe Smith replied.

"Come on over and we'll just do it," was John's answer.

It was as if an electric charge was working its way through the congregation.

Immediately the members noticed an increase in public responses. George Honeycutt's preaching developed an urgency, and an excitement transformed the singing. At the services that morning, George introduced two families with whom he had started Bible studies during the past week.

Two of the deacons were sitting in on the Bible studies with him so they could learn how to teach on their own. A small group of college students who had always sat together in the back corner asked the elders to help them start campus studies.

Paul Jr. began a Bible discussion group at school. They met for 30 minutes before school, and non-Christians were beginning to sit in on the classes.

Paul put an announcement on the bulletin board at work announcing the formation of a Bible study group during the Tuesday lunch hour in the conference room, and the first week, seven people came. Kathy mentioned her Mexico City experience to three of her neighbors, and they all voiced a desire to begin a neighborhood women's Bible study.

In a few weeks, the new life of the Central church began to attract the attention of the community. Visitors to their services were immediately invited to join one of the new study groups. Several members had started one-on-one evangelistic studies with relatives and close neighbors.

On a recent Sunday morning, eight new Bible studies with non-Christians were announced. The Jones' neighbors, Raul and Rene Hightower, were baptized. They were the tenth and eleventh to be converted. In only a few months, the congregation had matched the number of conversions during the last four years.

After years of smoldering, the hearts of these Christians had been rekindled. Their hearts were finally on fire.